The Age of Selfies

The Age of Selfies

Reasoning About Rights When the Stakes Are Personal

Adam J. MacLeod

ROWMAN & LITTLEFIELD
Lanham • Boulder • New York • London

Published by Rowman & Littlefield
An imprint of The Rowman & Littlefield Publishing Group, Inc.
4501 Forbes Boulevard, Suite 200, Lanham, Maryland 20706
www.rowman.com

6 Tinworth Street, London SE11 5AL, United Kingdom

British Library Cataloguing in Publication Information Available

Library of Congress Cataloging-in-Publication Data

ISBN 9781475854244 (cloth : alk. paper)
ISBN 9781475854251 (pbk. : alk. paper)
ISBN 9781475854268 (electronic)

♾ ™ The paper used in this publication meets the minimum requirements of American National Standard for Information Sciences Permanence of Paper for Printed Library Materials, ANSI/NISO Z39.48-1992.

To B. W. M. and G. C. N. W.,
who have taught me much about disagreeing well.

Contents

Preface

The motivation for this book is to learn how to reason together about our most important civic questions. Something has gone wrong with our public discourse. On that much, most people agree. But what to do about it?

Proposed solutions are all over the map. Many articles and books have appeared in recent years that lament our inability to reason together. Different authors have addressed many aspects of the problem. We have forgotten how to be civil toward each other, we lack civic friendship, and we do not communicate love and concern for each other. We hide behind anonymous Internet postings and social media; we seldom discuss our differences face-to-face, as neighbors. We accuse each other and attribute nefarious motives to each other rather than focus on the practical problems we can solve together.

These are all features of our public disagreements, and they impede our efforts to reason together and to persuade each other. However, the core of the problem is much simpler, more fundamental, and more difficult to remedy. Civic friendship, face-to-face conversations, concern for our local communities, and goodwill are all important. But what if our substantive differences are so radical that none of those virtues and practices are sufficient? Suppose that we are as divided today as Americans were in the nineteenth century about slavery and in the twentieth about civil rights, for the same reasons.

In short, suppose that we disagree about nonnegotiable principles. What then? If our differences concern not only policy, economics, and law but also go all the way down to what is right and wrong to do, then principled agreement might not be possible.

In fact, we do disagree about moral principles. When one listens carefully to what we are saying to each other, one sees that this is our situation. We express our disagreements in noncontingent, nonnegotiable claims about what is inherently just and inherently unjust to do. Moreover, the stakes could not be any more personal. We disagree both about what we should do and about who we are becoming as a people.

In the short term, it is difficult to see reasoned resolutions to all of our controversies that will satisfy everyone. Therefore, we might not be able to achieve consensus immediately. Perhaps we should start with a more modest goal. Maybe we should learn how to disagree well and productively, and then figure out how to live with our differences until we can reach agreement.

To do this, we need to relearn how to reason together about our common moral commitments in a culture that prioritizes the individual self. What afflicts our civic discourse is not only that we distrust each other (though that is a problem) or that social media encourages incivility (also a problem) or that we fail to see our political opponents as friends and fellow citizens (that too). We also suffer from our inability to reason together about what is right for us to do.

To some people, this might seem like a strange statement. Today, many people associate reason with scientific, economic, and similar empirical inquiries. They associate morals with religion, personal preferences, or purely individual commitments. But our actions show that we do want to reason together about moral problems because we fundamentally know that our moral disagreements are *reasoned* disagreements. Our contemporary discourse reveals that we think about moral controversies in rational terms, even though we are uncomfortable and unskilled at discussing them in rational terms.

In the abstract, we say that morals are personal. However, when we actually engage in discourse about justice and morality, we speak as if other people should agree with us. We try to reason with others, even those who disagree with us. In other words, by our actions, we demonstrate that we believe in right and wrong answers that everyone can access using their capacity to reason. Moreover, we reveal our conviction that those right and wrong answers are independent of personal belief or assent, that they are right and wrong even if our interlocutors disagree.

This revelation is the starting point for our recovery of civic discourse. We can (and should) examine our moral reasoning and learn what we can from it. We can, in short, revive moral education. And we can restore the role of moral education in the scheme of practical education generally. That is the beginning of the way forward.

For several decades now, moral instruction has been moved to the periphery of civic education. Our practical education is largely instrumental. We are taught skills and techniques that enable us to work more efficiently and effectively. We seldom stop to contemplate the point of it all, the most basic reasons why we do what we do. As a result, not many of us are trained or educated in moral discourse. We have not educated ourselves or our young people concerning how to think together about the most important issues underlying our civic controversies.

This book aims to correct that. It diagnoses the moral sources of our civic controversies. Moreover, it offers a prescription for recovering the ability to reason about fundamental, moral questions. It draws principles and lessons from different religious traditions and from the best liberal and conservative moral philosophy. It uses real-world and hypothetical examples to illustrate those principles and lessons. And it recommends heuristics and practices that can enable us to do moral education well.

Acknowledgments

I am grateful to those who helped bring this book into existence. Many teachers, friends, and mentors over the years have shown me how to think about rights and what is right to do and have modeled civil discourse about controversial questions. Tom Koerner at Rowman & Littlefield had a vision for a book about civic education before I did, and his persistence and encouragement were but-for causes of what follows (though none of the content should be attributed to him, and he should be held blameless for its flaws, especially the controversial flaws!). Nancy Bradley and Katie MacLeod identified mistakes in early drafts and graciously pointed out passages that required clarification, an act of love.

Introduction

Our most contentious disagreements today are moral disagreements. That is part of what makes them contentious. The stakes are high. Listen to our most prominent public figures, and you will hear not just political and economic terms but also *moral* language. We disagree not only about questions of efficiency and democracy and civil liberties but also about the meaning of more fundamental goods, such as personal autonomy, human life, and stewardship of nature. And we disagree not only about what to do but also about who we are becoming as people.

Yet these disagreements—these radical disagreements—might obscure an even more fundamental agreement. If we listen carefully to the different claims being made in the public square, we might find underlying our differences something that we hold common. The same public sentiments that show us to be divided on fundamental, moral questions also reveal that we think fundamental, moral principles are important. Moreover, our discourse shows that we want others to understand our moral concerns and to agree with us that they are important. In short, we disagree in moral terms because we agree that there are moral truths to be understood, reasoned about, and acted upon.

WE DISAGREE

Most of us want a civil and productive public discourse. However, we do not seem to know how to get there. Controversial, moral claims dominate public discourse about law and politics, and they are expressed in ways that seem to impede understanding and agreement. This makes some people uncomfortable. And even those who are comfortable discussing practical questions in moral terms often find it difficult to reason with people whose moral views are radically different.

On many issues—from abortion to religious liberty to environmental protection—our disagreements do seem quite intractable. Worse, we tend to express our disagreements in personal terms. We cannot convince each other at the level of ideas as long as we are debating who is the worst person among us. No one, no matter how tendentious his beliefs and vulnerable his ideas, will ever be persuaded by people who convey their belief that he is evil.

If we view our situation candidly—if we honestly acknowledge that many of our controversies are principled and intractable—then we can begin to move forward, for we can begin to understand each other. Let us begin with the premise that we argue so strenuously about right and wrong because we want to do what is right. How might that starting premise guide and shape our public discourse? It might reframe our discussions around our actual disagreements. Rather than assuming that our interlocutors are ignorant or uncaring or malevolent, we might come to see that we have reasoned disagreements about important, fundamental questions and that our moral disagreements are genuine. In other words, we might come to see that people can disagree in good faith.

We disagree quite radically about what is right to do. Yet we agree that there are right answers to our most pressing problems. Together, these two facts explain why even the most generous, knowledgeable, and level-headed people among us cannot seem to get very far in our efforts to reach agreement. Indeed, many people of goodwill today cannot even reach respectful disagreement. They think that other people are wrong about questions that matter, and they think that those other people should know better.

Consider abortion. Those who support legal rights to perform abortions and those who support the rights of the unborn hold views that cannot be reconciled to each other. All the goodwill in the world, all the desire to compromise that one can muster, cannot bridge the divide between the values at stake in this debate.

If the personal autonomy of the mother, in cooperation with her physician, is the most basic value, then the choice of the mother and abortionist must, in justice, prevail. If, on the other hand, human life is itself a basic value, then the value of any particular human life is not contingent on free choice (or any other factor), and an unwanted child is owed, in justice, as much legal protection as a wanted child. These views contradict each other not only in application and practice but also in principle. They stand opposed all the way down to the root.

This is not to suggest that the way in which we disagree with each other does not matter. We should pay attention to civic virtues. We should avoid ad hominem attacks. We should watch our tone, turn off our computers, and talk to each other. And we should, from time to time, set aside our differences and focus on what unites us so that we can cultivate friendships with those with whom we disagree. All of those practices are worthwhile and important. However, they are not enough.

We should not be surprised to find that our differences defy even our most charitable and best-informed efforts to reach consensus. We do not disagree merely about factual and pragmatic questions. We certainly have factual and pragmatic disagreements. Not everyone agrees when human life begins, for example. Moreover, even if we all agreed that abortion is morally problematic, there remains the difficult prudential question about what we should do about it. But our disagreements are more profound than these. We disagree about what makes free choice and human life valuable. No amount of scientific evidence or sophisticated policy planning can resolve that disagreement. On the abortion question, and many other issues of civic importance, evidence does not address the source of the disagreement.

Increasingly, we speak about public questions in moral terms. We act as if all reasonable people should agree with us, as if our opinions and expressions are right and others' opinions are wrong. That many of us speak and act as if moral and political questions have right and wrong answers indicates that, for all of our fractious disagreement, a consensus is emerging that there is moral truth—right and wrong—about the questions that occupy our public discourse. Once we get that clear in our minds, we can begin to progress toward more civil and productive disagreements. Indeed, we might even discover that we can reason together about what is to be done.

WE AGREE

We might hope to reason together because we agree on quite a lot. We agree that our controversies concern important questions. We agree that there are right and wrong answers to these questions. And, though we have not yet acknowledged this, we even agree about the nature of our disagreements. If we would listen to each other and to ourselves, if we would pay attention to the words we use and the values that we think are at stake, we would see that we think that our disagreements are moral disagreements and not empirical or scientific or pragmatic in nature.

That is our starting place. It may seem strange, but the profound nature of our disagreements is a reason to be hopeful. We are not apathetic. We care deeply about doing what is right and avoiding what is wrong. We demonstrate this concern by the moral terms we use to discuss abortion and climate change and religious liberty and equal protection of the laws and so on. Even among controversialists, we find common ground. Public figures today agree that there are moral obligations that human beings share and that should inform our public discourse.

We understand that the stakes are high, that these issues somehow concern not only our politics and our transactions but also our character, who we are as people, and who we will become. We care about ultimate things, the things that really matter. So we can look at those with whom we disagree and see in them people with whom we have the most important things in common.

What we are trying to do (though not very well at present) is to pursue a practical inquiry. We are trying to decide what we should do (and not do) about our most pressing problems. When we ask together, "What is right to do?", we discover that we are offering (different) answers to the same question and supplying different provisions for the same human need. We do not all agree on what is to be done. That is what divides us. But we all agree that it is important to know the answer. That is our common ground.

TOWARD HEALTHY DISAGREEMENT

In our educational, political, and legal institutions, moral ideals have for some decades been sidelined by neutral, political ideals such as democracy, liberty, and equality. These values that we all hold in common were supposed to be the basis for a sound and safe public discourse, in which we could meet and reason together free of moral controversies. As explained in Chapter 1 of this book, things have not turned out that way. The supposedly neutral public square now hosts deeply personal and openly moral rhetoric, accusations of moral failure, and even disparagement.

The demise of political neutrality is not cause for lament. It simply presents new challenges. Indeed, to have and express moral ideals is not a problem to solve but rather a reflection of what it means to be human. The problem is not that we think some things should be done and others not done. The problem is not even that we disagree. The problem is that we have lost the vocabulary and intellectual resources to achieve productive and civil disagreement. Instead, we merely find each other disagreeable.

This book aims to restore good and healthy disagreement in our discourse. The objective is not to make us all agree but to enable us to disagree well. The hope is that we will actually understand each other. If so, we might accept or reject the moral and political claims that we are making to each other on their own terms rather than assume that our opponents are ignorant or evil. Then we might live together in relative peace.

The moral nature of our public controversies has implications for how we go about civic discourse. We have not yet understood those implications well. We cannot reason together about what is right to do—we cannot even achieve reasoned disagreement—if we do not understand what we are saying to each other. Chapters 2 and 3 take a step toward the goal of mutual understanding. We look at different sources to find moral truth. To recognize that fact is to understand each other as moral beings, persons who care about the common good. Chapter 2 considers how some of those differences emerge in our efforts to do what is right and how we might better attribute correct motivations to each other. Further complicating our efforts to converse is that different generations use similar moral terms to refer to quite different ideals. Chapter 3 considers those differences so that we might bridge generational divides.

Chapters 4 and 5 frame a way to begin to reason together well. Rather than arguing about our controversies in the abstract, we can better focus on what is at stake when we ask a very practical question—call it the Practical Question—"What should I do?" To reframe our debates in practical, first-person terms is to clarify what we agree and disagree about and why it matters. It is also to see that we owe each other certain duties and obligations, and that the point of asserting claims of rights is to point us toward what is right to do. When we all take responsibility for the rights of ourselves and others, we begin to make progress toward doing what is right *together*.

To achieve genuine disagreement, we also must better understand the different sources of moral truth from which we are drawing. Chapter 6 takes up that task. When we compare these sources, we come to see that they sometimes conflict, but not perhaps as often as we assume. Moreover, we come to see that none of us is completely innocent. As explained in Chapter 8, the recognition that we all contribute to moral confusion might lead us to approach our controversies more humbly and with greater charity toward others.

If we can wrap our minds around the different sources of moral truth, then we might also understand our different situations, goals, and judgments. We might find that we can safely agree to disagree on many important questions while also honoring the rights of each other, a possibility taken up in stages in Chapters 5, 7, and 9. We might even build a principled, plural order in society in which we can live comfortably with disagreement where we may disagree and achieve agreement on those things that we must agree upon to preserve our society. That is the proposal set out in Chapter 10. We can learn how to avoid one-size-fits-all solutions and allow the common good of everyone to flourish in all its diverse aspects, even as we insist that no one may infringe on the absolute rights of others.

The main text of this book stops there. For those who are willing to venture a little farther, the postscript goes on to propose a more challenging and more fruitful way to live well together. It is known as forgiveness. Some people may balk at that way and will not want to travel that far. No matter how far you are willing to travel with me through this book, I am grateful for your willingness to come along.

ONE

The Return of Morals
(and the End of Neutrality)

THE AGE OF MORALITY

We live in an age of morals. We have controversies aplenty. And many of us think that we should look to moral imperatives to resolve them. Everywhere one turns, someone is talking about our political and cultural issues in terms of what we should and should not do. Moreover, they are using words such as "right," "wrong," "good," and "evil."

It was not always this way. We have always had controversies. However, we have not always discussed or resolved them as we do now. Until recently, our discourse about important civic issues was full of words such as "efficient," "effective," and "democratic." Moral ideas were considered private. Public discourse was supposed to be neutral ground where we solved our problems and resolved our differences on the basis of shared political ideals, scientific and economic evidence, and common commitments.

Until recently, most people thought of our rights as *political* rights, our obligations as *legal* obligations, on which we all generally agreed. Everyone was entitled to a presumption of liberty and equal protection of the laws. No one was to be subjected to legal sanction or liability who did not commit a culpable wrong that was clearly forbidden by law. It was thought that no one should face censure or bullying for expressing an opinion, even if the views he expressed were unpopular. A strong sense prevailed that no one should be required to act contrary to her conscience. But as long as our controversies were decided by democratic deliberation and neutral proceedings, we all were expected to accept the results, even if we disagreed with them. Those civil and political commit-

1

ments were thought to secure the public square as a place where we could work out our differences on neutral ground.

If there ever really was such a public place of neutrality, it is no longer. The civil liberties that marked the boundaries of the public square are eroding. And for all of our differences, we have this in common: More of us think and speak in terms of right and wrong than our recent predecessors. Progressives, social conservatives, and libertarians increasingly use moral words in their public discourse. Moreover, they use those words for the same purpose—to advocate for actions. Increasingly, we identify our rights and liberties not with what we have and possess but instead with what is right *to do*. Many of us are willing to critique political rights and legal duties in moral terms.

For example, a Democratic Congresswoman who advocates for Socialist ideals thinks that it is most important for politicians to be "morally right."[1] "Morally right about what?", you might ask. Well, nearly *everything*. For example, she has said the following:

> The question of marginal tax rates is a policy question but it's also a moral question. What kind of society do we want to live in? Are we comfortable with a society where someone can have a personal helipad while this city is experiencing the highest levels of poverty and homelessness since the Great Depression? . . . I'm not saying that Bill Gates or Warren Buffet are immoral, but a system that allows billionaires to exist when there are parts of Alabama where people are still getting ringworm because they don't have access to public health is wrong.[2]

She has also suggested that it is morally wrong to have children.

> Our planet is going to hit disaster if we don't turn this ship around, and so it's basically, like, there's a scientific consensus that the lives of children are going to be very difficult. And it does lead, I think, young people to have a legitimate question, you know, "Is it okay to still have children?". . . . Like, we need a universal sense of urgency, and people are, like, trying to introduce watered-down proposals that are frankly going to kill us. A lack of urgency is going to kill us.[3]

The same tendencies can be seen at the other end of the political spectrum. A former Republican state Chief Justice and US Senate candidate founded a think tank called the "Foundation for Moral Law," which advocates for public displays of the Ten Commandments, "the basis of our virtue and morality."[4] Most of the positions of his Senate campaign are expressed as moral imperatives.

- "We should not be entangled in foreign wars merely at the whim and caprice of a President."
- "America should serve as a good example to other nations."
- "We must treat sovereign nations as we would want to be treated and stand with allies to protect and preserve our national security."

- "Churches and charitable organizations should be encouraged to help the needy and poor."
- "A strong family based on marriage between one man and one woman is and should remain our only guide and model. I oppose abortion, same-sex marriage, civil unions, and all other threats to the traditional family order."
- "We must remain a moral and virtuous people, 'One Nation under God.'" [5]

These two public figures disagree on many issues. However, they agree on the centrality of right and wrong to our civic discourse. Notice all the uses of "should" and "must," "moral" and "immoral." These are not appeals to neutral principles. The claim is not that we all agreed on these propositions, nor that the propositions were settled by democratic processes that are fair to all. Instead, the claim is that any person who is thinking clearly about what should be done would agree that these propositions are true and ought to be acted upon.

Notice also the intellectual consistency. Both of these public figures have comprehensive views of what is right and wrong and how to tell the difference. They are principled. And their success indicates that many Americans want principled solutions to our problems. Each of these public figures enjoys political support in his or her home state because many other Americans also agree that we should do what is morally right and not do what is morally wrong.

At the same time, our discourse is becoming more personal. Our disagreements are moral, and our moral differences are seen as extensions of our personalities. Many people describe what is right for them in terms of personal identity. And they describe other people's wrongs, failures, and mistakes in terms of personal defects. To reject a person's views and opinions is, therefore, seen not only as a rejection of their ideas but also as a rejection of the person.

Together, these trends make our civil discourse both promising and difficult. Moral discourse has advantages and disadvantages with respect to other kinds of discourse. On the positive side, our moral discourse emphasizes personal responsibility. Moreover, it enables us to talk about the things that matter most to us. Whatever the majority thinks, whatever the law provides, we can consider the fundamental issues and real goods at stake in our problems and controversies—goods such as personal autonomy, human life, virtue, conservation of the natural environment, integrity, charity, and concern for others.

Furthermore, the sharp edges of moral discourse often help us to see matters clearly. More pragmatic forms of discourse, such as discussions about policy, politics, and business judgments, tend to be nuanced and contingent upon circumstances. By contrast, moral discourse is often simple, clear, and universal. Moral claims are accessible and unequivocal.

They tell us what to do and what not to do in terms that we all can understand and act upon.

Moral discourse also helps us better see the boundaries around our choices and actions. The point of making a moral claim is to assert what is right to do, regardless of context and consequences. That is an important feature of moral claims because some actions are ones that we should never be willing to do, no matter how much benefit we might gain. For example, we should never be willing to maim, rape, or enslave. Period.

Moral discourse, therefore, helps us to clarify things that matter. However, with this clarity comes a danger. Many practical questions facing us today are not so simple. Reasonable minds disagree about many important issues. And where a practical question admits more than one reasonable answer, to make a moral claim can be a way to cheat, to end what should be a longer and more detailed conversation. It can also be a way to disparage one's opponents.

Moral claims are tempting because they are a superior kind of normative currency. Over and against pragmatic considerations, a moral claim is a sort of trump card. To say, "This is the right thing to do," is to say that other ways are wrong. Maybe they are wrong. However, we should have reasons to think so. We should not rule out of bounds alternative opinions, choices, and ways of life that are reasonable just because the loudest moralist condemns them in categorical terms.

Furthermore, our moralistic expressions today are often personal, even self-righteous. Moral arguments often concern not only ideas but also character. They address what is right and wrong to do and so contain implicit (or even explicit) judgments about wrong actions. And because wrong actions are performed by people, including many of the people engaged in moral discourse, moral claims imply personal judgments.

As a result, moral discourse often devolves into personal condemnation. It is tethered to a temptation to make every issue personal. Increasingly, we condemn each other not only as misguided or wrong, but also as unjust, shameful, or even bad people.

AN EXAMPLE: ABORTION

Consider one example. Controversy erupted after the State of New York enacted a law extending legal protections for abortion until just before birth. Shortly thereafter, the legislature of Georgia passed—and the governor later signed into law—a bill to restrict access to abortions after a fetal heartbeat. These enactments motivated dramatic, public moral claims.

The Georgia statute prohibits physicians from performing all abortions after a heartbeat can be detected in an unborn infant, except in cases where the child was conceived in rape or incest or where the life of the mother is in danger. Supporters of the law believe that unborn infants are morally indistinguishable from born infants, and they are, therefore, persons who deserve legal protection from intentional killing. They argue that an abortionist who performs an abortion after a heartbeat is detected is committing an act of murder.

Many opponents of the Georgia law do not deny that abortion is morally problematic. They simply think that the immorality of some abortions is irrelevant. They argue that the moral status of abortion is not a valid consideration on which lawmakers may justly predicate restrictions on abortion because women have a constitutional right to access abortions. The decision whether to have an abortion, therefore, belongs to a woman and her physicians.

This is a standard type of argument in legal and political discourse. It is an argument from neutral principles; in this case, civil liberties. The constitutions and laws of many societies permit—and even secure civil liberties to perform—actions that majorities believe are immoral and actions that are immoral in fact. For example, lying is immoral. However, the law provides no remedy for lies told except in a few categories of especially harmful lies, such as a lie that is told under oath (i.e., perjury) or that defames someone. The law also tolerates drunkenness, adultery, and other immoral acts (except to the extent that they cause or threaten to cause public harm). Law and morality are not the same thing in societies that honor civil liberties. Therefore, moral arguments are not alone sufficient to justify restrictive laws.

Nevertheless, not all opponents of the Georgia heartbeat law objected on neutral principles or grounds of civil liberties. Some prominent political and cultural figures instead asserted that the law is not merely unconstitutional but immoral. In particular, a former Speaker of the Georgia House of Representatives and a candidate for governor called the new law "abominable and evil."[6]

As this rhetoric illustrates, the abortion debate is no longer confined to neutral reasons (if it ever was), such as civil liberties and democracy. Each side in this debate believes that the other side's views and proposals are not just misguided but evil. Each side believes that it is objectively right and its opponents are objectively wrong. To say that someone's view is "evil" is not merely to say that one disagrees with it or that one is not persuaded by it. Rather, it is to suppose that there is some objective standard of right and wrong that the speaker knows and *his opponent also knows*. And judged by that standard, the opponent's view is not simply illogical or unpleasant but morally false. It is outside the range of what can reasonably be accepted.

Now discussions veer dangerously toward the personal. These accusations also might imply defects of character. For example, the former Georgia House Speaker opined that the Georgia abortion law is not only "bad for business" but also "bad for morality and our humanity."[7] The implication is that those who support legal protections for the unborn fail not only in respect of their thinking but also in respect of their moral agency. They fail to recognize and respect the humanity of those who seek and perform abortions. They fail to act as humans should act because they fail to extend the same moral respect to others that they expect for themselves.

The accusation is not well-founded. Supporters of abortion restrictions have moral and factual reasons to believe that unborn human beings are persons who deserve legal protection. Whether or not their view is correct, the Georgia politician failed to account for her opponents' reasons and the sincerity of the people who act on them. Indeed, she committed precisely the error she attributed to her opponents—a failure to respect the humanity of some people, namely pro-lifers.

However, she is not wrong to worry that holding a wrong view can endanger one's moral integrity. In certain circumstances, holding a false moral view can make someone a morally worse-off person. For example, a person becomes racist by affirming and maintaining the view that other people of a different race do not deserve civil liberties. A person becomes a eugenicist by affirming and maintaining the view that some lives are not worthy of being lived.

Making and accepting immoral arguments can have a corrosive effect on the character and judgment of the person who articulates the arguments. One who advocates for murder or enslavement becomes somehow like a murderer or slave owner. We have witnessed this in our history when those who rationalized slavery became the kind of people who could rationalize lynches and segregation. Some people develop the habit of thinking wrongly about others by accepting views that they should know are wrong.

Many people in the abortion debate think that something similar is happening to their opponents. Advocates of abortion rights express concern that some opponents of abortion have become misogynistic. Advocates of pro-life laws express concern that many abortionists have grown immune to the brutalities of the practice.

However, we must be careful with accusations such as these, for we might not really understand the motivations of our interlocutors. (More on that possibility in the next chapter.) Furthermore, not everyone who holds false moral views does so because of a moral failure. People might believe moral falsehoods from a failure of reason, integrity, or character. Some people want to rationalize wrong conduct. But they might also be innocent. People hold false views who are uninformed, biased, or confused. They are not bad people or willfully self-deceived. They just do not fully understand.

Nevertheless, the concern remains. These debates are not simply political or legal. They concern what kind of people we should be and what kind of people we are becoming. Participants in the debate are concerned with legal justice and the rule of law. They care about political and legal principles of liberty and equality. They *also* worry that advocating for evil and unjust laws is causing their opponents to become unjust, even evil.

THE END OF NEUTRALITY

As the abortion controversy illustrates, we are talking about ideals that matter. But we are not expressing them very well. Our public discourse is full of scolding moralism. We don't understand each other very well, but many of us seem quite sure that we know what is best for other people.

At the same time, our politics are falling apart. Our public life together has long been thought to be governed by neutral principles of democracy, political and civil liberties, and equal protection of the law. We have long trusted our political ideals and institutions to resolve our differences on neutral grounds. We have expected our political institutions to mediate between people and groups of people on grounds of ideals that we all share in common rather than religion, morals, and other controversial grounds.

Today, consensus on political principles and trust in political institutions are unraveling. The ideal of neutrality seems to have failed. We see neutral ground disappearing on university campuses and on cable television, on both the Right and the Left. People are becoming more tribal, more fractious, and more distrustful of political institutions and public powers. We do not trust our neighbors to hold political power, to educate our children, or to make important decisions in our civic and cultural institutions.

A recent public controversy illustrates the problem. A debacle ensued when Google announced the launch of an ethics board to guide its "responsible development" of artificial intelligence, known as "AI."[8] This admirable effort by Google was aimed at one of the most pressing problems of our time. It failed before it got started.

Many of the decisions that affect our lives that used to be made by human beings are now made by AI. How to develop AI responsibly is a big question. According to a report, Google's concerns "include how AI can enable authoritarian states, how AI algorithms produce disparate outcomes, whether to work on military applications of AI, and more." AI is a powerful tool that can be used for good or evil. Google did well to commission a diverse board of accomplished thinkers to consider how to prevent AI from violating our basic commitments.

Within days of Google's announcement about its advisory board, members of the board began to resign over fundamental moral disagreements. Some board members also complained that Google had not committed to provide adequate time and resources to facilitate meaningful deliberation. However, the most notorious conflict on the board concerned two, irreconcilable moral views.

One of the board members appointed is the president of a conservative think tank called the Heritage Foundation. She and the organization she heads hold the view that men and women are different and are not interchangeable. And she has publicly expressed concern that ratifying the gender identities of men who identify as women might harm the equal rights of women. If men can change their gender to female then they might deprive women of opportunities, perhaps even political equality.

Some people hold the view that sex should not determine a person's gender identity, that a biological male must have the right to identify as a woman and be treated like a woman. Reflecting this view, a couple of thousand people signed a petition to have the Heritage Foundation president removed from Google's advisory board because they deemed her views morally illegitimate. By appointing her to the advisory board, "Google elevates and endorses her views, implying that hers is a valid perspective worthy of inclusion in its decision making," the petition asserts. "This is unacceptable."[9]

This charge left Google no neutral ground on which to stand. Neither Heritage Foundation nor its president violated anyone's liberty or equality in the classic sense of those ideals. They are not motivated by hate or animus toward any class of persons. To the contrary, many people who hold the view that male and female are determined by human nature are motivated to challenge transgender notions by their concern for others.

The Heritage Foundation president has a radically different view of human nature and sexuality than her critics. She views transgender identity as inherently incompatible with a correct understanding of human nature. And she views it as potentially incompatible with equal rights for women. She was willing to serve on Google's board and to discourse with people who disagree. However, she could not in conscience affirm something about human nature she believes to be false or to deny something she understands to be true.

From the perspective of her critics, her views of human nature are morally illicit, like the views of racists. To those who hold the view that transgender identity is a moral right, to allow someone to participate in Google's ethical deliberations who holds the view that men and women are inherently different is to give that view more credence than it deserves. It does not matter that she harbors no ill will toward others. The effect of her expressed views is that she refuses to affirm the gender identity of members of the transgender community. This is what they view as intolerance, and this sort of intolerance cannot be tolerated.

These competing views cannot be reconciled; they are inherently incompatible. They are like "x" and "not-x," existence and nonexistence. They cannot both be affirmed. And both views are sincerely held. Some people really believe that a woman is biologically a woman, and others really believe that a woman might be trapped in a male body.

As this controversy demonstrates, our profound differences cannot be resolved simply by being nice to each other and appealing to neutral principles. We must take account of the radical fissures in our moral and civic discourse. We disagree not only on pragmatic considerations, such as efficiency and fair processes but also on first principles. We still agree that people must be secure in their equal political and civil liberties. However, we disagree about what those principles mean. We disagree about the importance of life and autonomy. We disagree about what it means to be male and female. And many people think that on such questions of principle, compromise is not possible.

Until recently, we seemed to have a general consensus about our basic commitments. We would have expressed them as political and legal principles of liberty and equality. The principle of liberty meant that everyone is presumed innocent and left alone to live their lives. No one may be subjected to imprisonment or other liability unless and until they are proven to have committed a legal wrong. One implication of this principle might be that Google should not develop AI to enable its misuse by law enforcement.

The principle of equality meant that everyone is entitled to equal protection of the laws and public officials should not discriminate against people based on immutable, personal characteristics, such as race and religious conviction, but only on the basis of choices and actions. One implication might be that AI should not be used for racial profiling by insurance companies.

That consensus has now unraveled. Many people now think that liberty is not merely a political principle but also a moral principle. It means not only that everyone should be presumed innocent and left alone to live their lives but also that everyone should have as many opportunities in life as possible. Whereas under the older idea of liberty, it was enough simply to leave other people alone, under this new idea of liberty, some people have obligations to provide opportunities for other people.

The principle of equality also has changed into something less neutral and more demanding. Unlawful discrimination used to mean *intentional* discrimination. Thus, one could avoid violating the principle of equality simply by ignoring other people's personal traits, such as race. As long as we made decisions about others based on their choices and actions, it didn't matter what race they were, what convictions they espoused, or how they identified.

Now, many people think that equality has an affirmative component. It is not enough to avoid discriminating against others intentionally. Now one has an obligation to ensure that one's decisions do not have disparate *effects* on others. Therefore, someone who makes a decision without regard to race might be held responsible for racial discrimination if racial minorities are (unintentionally) affected by the decision in disproportionate numbers. Equality is taken to mean not only equality of respect but also equality of result.

In these ways, even our basic commitments to liberty and equality have become controversial. These controversies are not easily brushed aside. They arise out of radical differences concerning who we are as people and what we owe each other. They are moral controversies. And they are unavoidable.

WE NEED A NEW SETTLEMENT

In sum, neutral ground has disappeared because our neutral principles are themselves contested. We disagree sharply on the moral commitments on which our political principles rest. Therefore, the solution to the collapse of political neutrality is not to prop up the crumbling edifice. It is rather to build a new settlement, one that respects and takes account of moral obligations. We must reason together about what we owe each other. As we talk about what is right to do, we should pay close attention to what is good and true. We must relearn *how* to reason together about what is right.

Consider again the controversy that precipitated the collapse of Google's ethics panel. We make a mistake if we think that our differences over gender identity are merely political. Indeed, it is patronizing to say so. The person who thinks that the sex one is assigned at birth is arbitrary and the person who thinks that sex is a biological and inherent aspect of personal dignity have principled and irreconcilable *reasons* to believe as they do.

As long as we value civil liberties—and may we always value civil liberties—many people will insist that they should have freedom of sexual expression, including the freedom to express a gender identity that does not correspond to one's biological sex. And as long as there are men and women—and may there always be men and women—many people will believe that men and women are different in important ways, constituted as male or female by nature, and not interchangeable with each other.

These differences are not going away. And when these convictions are applied to various controversies about sex-segregated sports, bathroom facilities, and other matters of civic importance, the judgments that follow from them will be inherently irreconcilable. This is true not only of controversies about transgender identity but also of controversies about environmental protection and economic regulation, tax policy and freedom of contract, and other pressing, public questions.

On any number of important civic questions—from abortion to how the law should define marriage, to climate change and gender identity, to whether the government should subsidize public transportation—people hold opposing views. Moreover, they hold those views as a matter of principle. They are opposed to each other not simply because they are churlish and can't get along (though that is sometimes the case) but also because they believe that people on the other side are objectively and radically wrong in an important respect.

TOWARD A NEW SETTLEMENT: ORDERED LIBERTY, EQUAL DIGNITY, AND MORAL IDEALS

Do not despair. Political neutrality failed us, but it was never the source of liberty and equality anyway. Our civil rights and liberties do not depend first and foremost on politics. They are more basic than that (as we will see in later chapters). To the extent that we have gotten along peacefully and learned to respect equal rights, something more fundamental than politics has been doing the work. Put not your trust in princes, nor in the ballot box.

Political neutrality does not deserve the credit for our peace and prosperity any more than it deserves blame for totalitarianism. The moral atrocities of the twentieth century were perpetrated by societies committed to ideals of democracy and equality. The Nazis achieved political power democratically. The Soviets and their client states murdered tens of millions of people in pursuit of their stated goals to reduce inequality. They made everyone equally poor (except the ruling elite). Tyrants hijack political ideals just as they can hijack moral and religious ideals.

Furthermore, political ideals are not the most fundamental source of equality and ordered liberty. Political ideals cannot work unless we first understand what we owe each other. To say that we ought to respect each other's liberty is to beg the question of what liberty is. That is a moral question. To say that we ought to be equal is to beg the question in what sense we must be equal and what sort of differences are tolerable. Those are also moral questions.

The political ideals that we are supposed to hold in common turn out to be illusory unless we understand them as secondary to more fundamental, moral ideals. We have always had our differences. In the United States and in Europe, in the Middle East and Africa, neighbors live alongside neighbors of different tribes, ethnicities, religions, and political ambitions. Not all of them live together peacefully. If we have sometimes trusted our political institutions and ideals to resolve our differences then that is because we have believed that our neighbors would peacefully relinquish power when they lost the next election and that they would not use their power to deprive us of our rights in the interim. Something motivated that restraint. It was not politics. What was it?

We get a clue if we look at the moments when neighbors proved unworthy of each other's trust. Consider racial segregation in South Africa and the American South. We think that Apartheid and Jim Crow were profoundly unjust. However, the fundamental reason they were unjust is not that segregationists violated principles of democracy. Rather, what made segregation unjust is that segregationists used political power to treat human beings as less than fully human. They acted immorally. Their actions would have been no less unjust had they assiduously adhered to democratic principles. The tyranny of the majority is still tyranny.

Civil rights activists understood this. When Martin Luther King Jr. sat in a jail cell in Birmingham, Alabama, to call attention to the injustice of segregation, the famous letter he penned did not recite a litany of political abuses. It described moral wrongs. King appealed to a moral law, a law that every person knows and that the most powerful officials cannot erase from the minds and hearts of human beings. As we will see, that law is the secure foundation of our ordered liberty and equal worth. To understand it is to see why moral claims now dominate our public discourse. And it is to begin to understand how to converse with each other in a civil and productive way.

NOTES

1. Transcript of Interview with Alexandria Ocasio-Cortez, CBS News (January 6, 2019), https://www.cbsnews.com/news/alexandria-ocasio-cortez-the-rookie-congress-woman-challenging-the-democratic-establishment-60-minutes-interview-full-transcript-2019-01-06/?ftag=CNM-00-10aab7d&linkId=62017632.

2. Mikhael Smits, "Ocasio-Cortex Calls Existence of Billionaires 'Immoral,'" *Washington Free Beacon* (January 22, 2019), https://freebeacon.com/politics/ocasio-cortez-calls-existence-of-billionaires-immoral/.

3. Ryan Saavedra, "Ocasio-Cortez: People Maybe Shouldn't Reproduce Due to Climate Change," *Daily Wire* (February 25, 2019), https://www.dailywire.com/news/43880/ocasio-cortez-people-maybe-shouldnt-reproduce-due-ryan-saavedra.

4. Statement of Faith, Foundation for Moral Law, http://morallaw.org/about/statement-of-faith/; Defending the Monument, Foundation for Moral Law, http://morallaw.org/about/defending-the-monument/.

5. https://www.roymoore.org/Positions/.

6. Benjamin Gill, "GA Dem Called Heartbeat Bill 'Abominable and Evil,' 'Bad for Morality,' Implying Abortion Is Morally Superior," *Christian Broadcasting Network* (April 10, 2019), https://www1.cbn.com/cbnnews/us/2019/april/ga-dem-actually-called-heartbeat-bill-abominable-and-evil-and-bad-for-morality-implying-abortion-is-morally-superior-to-life.

7. Calvin Freiburger, "Dem Stacey Abrams claims it's 'evil' for Georgia to protect babies with beating hearts," *Life Site News* (April 9, 2019), https://www.lifesitenews.com/news/dem-stacey-abrams-claims-its-evil-for-georgia-to-protect-babies-with-beating-hearts.

8. Kelsey Piper, "Google's brand-new AI ethics board is already falling apart," *Vox* (April 3, 2019).

9. "Googlers Against Transphobia and Hate," https://medium.com/@against.transphobia/googlers-against-transphobia-and-hate-b1b0a5dbf76.

TWO
Understanding Each Other

We are rational animals. Human beings are unique in this sense. We have appetites and passions and desires, just like other animals. However, we also possess the radically unique capacity to choose and act for reasons. We are capable of behaving irrationally. But each of us has the capacity to understand what is good and right to do, and then we can choose to do it.

We do not all develop this ability in equal measure. Nor do we always exercise the ability when we have it. Sometimes we choose what is unreasonable and not good for us, even when we know better. (Who hasn't gone back for a second slice of cake, snuck a midnight snack of cookies, or done something at least as unwise?) However, every human being is the kind of being who has the capacity to act rationally.

This means, among other things, that every person you encounter is an agent of reason and reasoned choice. Every person you encounter is worthy of respect as a rational agent. Even people whose thinking has gone wrong in important and destructive ways—even slave owners and murderers—are the kind of beings who have the capacity to reason and be reasoned with: *human* beings.

Most of us do not go wrong as dramatically as the slave owner or murderer. However, all of us are capable of error, just as we are capable of knowing and reasoning about the truth. (More on that in Chapter 8.) Yet we never lose our intrinsic status as human beings, nor our capacity for reasoned action. Therefore, we are all entitled to respect, even when we go wrong in our thinking. Furthermore, that a person has gone wrong in some aspect of their thought does not entail that they are wrong about everything. We might learn something from those with whom we disagree because they might know things that we do not know, or understand better in some respect what is to be done, even if they misunderstand in other respects, or do what we know to be wrong.

So, we should reason together. Each of us is entitled to respect as an agent of reason, and each of us has knowledge that we can impart to others, just as each of us goes wrong in some respects and is ignorant of certain truths. Before we can be certain about what is to be done, we need to understand each other. We need to understand what each of us is saying to others. As a bonus, when we understand each other, we will better understand ourselves.

Unfortunately, the public discourse that we witness too often today is not aimed at understanding each other's reasons. Nor is it designed to engage the merits of our controversies. It is instead uncivil and unproductive. The people who receive the most attention in our public discourse seem mostly interested in attacking those who disagree with them, in scoring cheap debater's points by attributing nefarious motivations to their critics, and, in general, distracting from the real issues and fomenting distrust. They make public discourse personal.

This coarsening of our public discourse goes all the way to the top of our society. The forty-fourth president of the United States infamously referred to people whom he expected to vote against him as "bitter" people who "cling to guns or religion or antipathy to people who aren't like them or anti-immigrant sentiment."[1] He frequently attributed the worst imaginable motivations to his critics. Unfortunately, his successor, the forty-fifth president, has taken this game to a new level entirely, adding profanity to his frequent personal attacks on those who criticize him or disagree with his proposals.[2]

These tendencies extend well beyond the Oval Office of the American White House. The *New York Times*, America's most influential newspaper, reported recently about itself that it "found it fit to print the B.S. word just 14 times in the many years before Mr. Trump's inauguration, according to a Nexis search, but has used it 26 times since—not all in stories covering the president."[3] Moreover, even stories that are not profane are often unnecessarily divisive. Most left-liberals do not recognize themselves in the descriptions of liberals that they hear on talk radio, just as conservatives do not recognize themselves in descriptions of conservatives that they hear on National Public Radio or read in the *New York Times*.

The resources and technologies available to us, and the leisure time we have on our hands, give us unprecedented power to communicate our views, opinions, and ideas. And those of us who are fortunate enough to live in free societies enjoy civil liberties of speech and expression that most of the people who have lived throughout history could not even have dreamed of. We do not often enough stop to consider how we are exercising this power and freedom. Not enough of us exercise it responsibly, for the common good of all.

FOUR MORALISTS

If we are going to get anywhere in our discourse, then we must move beyond stereotypes and personal attacks. We must stop attributing to each other the worst motivations. We must instead seek to understand the reasonable, even admirable, motivations of people with whom we disagree.

Consider the following four people. Let's call them the four moralists. Each has principled reasons to believe that certain things should be done and other things must not be done. However, their principles seem to conflict with the principles held by the others. Indeed, their judgments and proposals even contradict each other on some points.

These four moralists represent four types. They are, of course, caricatures. However, they are not stereotypes. Indeed, each defies a common stereotype. Each possesses characteristics of real persons who commonly express their opinions on matters of civic importance today. And each acts on motivations that other people miss. We need to understand those motivations better.

Reese Cycler

Reese is a responsible guy. He takes good care of his possessions. He has been wearing some of the same T-shirts since high school, not because he is afraid to spend money on new ones but because the old ones haven't worn out yet, and he sees nothing to be gained by throwing them away.

Reese cuts his lawn each week with a push mower. He picks up trash that people leave on the street where he lives. He pays his taxes gladly and on time. He does his job well. He shows up for work on time every morning. He often finishes his own tasks ahead of schedule and is willing and able to help others complete their tasks before he leaves work for home.

Reese has the same sense of responsibility for the natural environment that he has for his material possessions and his vocation. He appreciates how fortunate we are to live on planet Earth. He understands that we only have one such planet and that we have no guarantee of finding another. He believes very strongly that we ought to take care of the planet that we have. And he believes that we owe it to future generations not to consume more than our fair share of natural resources.

Reese is not a scientist. However, he regularly reads accounts of scientific studies in the popular press and is troubled that more people are not paying attention to the findings of those studies. He is especially concerned about global warming and climate change and is persuaded that human activities are causing significant and potentially catastrophic changes to the planet's atmosphere and ecosystems.

Reese believes that we all have a moral obligation to reduce our consumption, especially of fossil fuels. He believes that this obligation is an immediate imperative. If people will not cut back consumption voluntarily, then Reese thinks that the laws should be changed to make it harder and more expensive to travel by airplane and automobile, to own large houses, and to have large families.

Contrary to stereotype, Reese is not a radical tree-hugger. Nor is he a Socialist, Malthusian, or eugenicist. He attended a couple of protests in college but has since made his peace with free markets, libertarians, and fossil fuels. He accepts that people have different views than he. However, he does what he can to model environmental responsibility in his own life. And he votes and advocates publicly for candidates and legal reforms that might curb what he perceives to be the excesses of a consumption society.

Lawson Order

Lawson obeys the law. When he gets behind the wheel, Lawson buckles his seatbelt and drives the speed limit and comes to a complete stop at each stop sign. As an active member of several civic groups in his community, Lawson frequently instructs other people about what the rules require and allow. He attends neighborhood association and city council meetings regularly. He reads the news each morning and takes note of crime trends.

Lawson keeps his promises. He only makes promises that he intends to keep. He is as dependable as the Rock of Gibraltar.

In short, Lawson plays by the book. He strongly believes that everyone else should do the same. Indeed, he attributes much of the societal breakdown about which he reads in the news to a ready willingness of many people to break the law. He believes that rule-breaking is a kind of cheating. Someone who lives in a lawful and orderly society enjoys the benefits of law and order. To reap the benefits of law and order while flouting the law is morally the same as stealing from one's fellow citizens.

Lawson believes that it is a great privilege to live in a nation that has the rule of law. For this reason, he is deeply troubled by illegal immigration. His view is that a person who comes into a country without satisfying the legal requirements is demonstrating disrespect to the citizens, lawful residents, and legal immigrants of that country. He thinks that immigration law enforcement should be the first priority of the national executive, right alongside national defense. Indeed, he thinks that enforcing immigration laws is an essential aspect of the executive's obligation to preserve both fairness and national security.

Contrary to stereotype, Lawson is not a racist or a xenophobe. He would be just as happy to welcome law-abiding immigrants from any country and of any ethnicity. And he is not opposed in principle to immigration reform. However, he thinks that any sensible immigration law should be enforced and that any sensible reform must preserve the rule of law.

I. Denti Tarian

Denti identifies as a cis-gendered, heterosexual female. In other words, she has XX chromosomes, her birth certificate says she is female, she identifies as female, and she is attracted to men. However, she does not think that her identity is inherently normative for anyone else. She believes that some women—people who are truly female—happen to have male DNA and genitalia. She thinks that the romantic love between two women or two men is just as admirable and worthwhile as the love between a cis-gendered woman and a cis-gendered man.

Denti believes that gender and marriage are social constructs rather than natural realities or moral obligations. She thinks that only ignorance and bigotry could lead anyone to the conclusion that a person with XX chromosomes must behave like a "woman" and a person with XY chromosomes must behave like a "man." Similarly, only narrow minds would limit marital status to man-woman unions or refuse to affirm the love between two people of the same sex.

Though she is cis-gendered and heterosexual, Denti both sympathizes and empathizes with people who experience minority sexual-orientation and gender identities. She was often bullied in school and remembers the pain of being ostracized for being different. She feels very strongly that everyone should be affirmed for being who they are and that no one should feel pressure to fit in, to conform to cultural stereotypes, or to meet others' expectations or satisfy others' preferences.

Contrary to stereotype, Denti is not a snowflake. Nor is she particularly angry. She recognizes that other people hold different views. However, she thinks they are wrong. Moreover, she believes that they are wrong because they are bigoted. If they only would get to know differently oriented and differently gendered people, then their moral objections would evaporate like snow on a sunny day. She thinks the evilest thing is to live contrary to one's feelings and experience. She spends her time teaching people how to be authentic and to avoid inner tensions and concern for the opinions of others. And she advocates for laws that require people to affirm minority sexual orientations and gender identities.

Dee Vine Leeledd

Dee attends religious services at least once every week. She reads the Bible every morning, and she spends much of the day listening to religious music and programming on the radio. She is consistently cheerful, even when life is difficult and things are not going her way. She is a friend to those in need and often spends her weekends and holidays serving in homeless shelters and other ministries to the poor. Though she lives on a fixed income, she gives away more than 10 percent of her income to her church and to other charitable ventures, including organizations that provide aid to poor communities overseas.

Dee does all of these things because she believes that it pleases God. She believes in the existence of a personal God who created everything that is good. She believes that she owes God her obedience to His commands, which are expressed in the Bible and in the authoritative teachings of the church she attends.

Dee believes that everyone would be better off if they were simply to obey God's commands. Indeed, she believes that disobedience to or ignorance of God's commands is a sort of rebellion against one's creator and, therefore, an act of violence toward one's own nature. No person can have true joy and contentment as long as they remain in rebellion against God. She thinks that many people are anxious and discontent because they are trying to live their lives for themselves rather than for God. Furthermore, she believes that the nation as a whole is accountable to God and that true justice cannot be achieved until the people are obedient to God's law.

Contrary to stereotype, Dee does not want to impose her views on others by coercion or force. She is neither a scolder nor a theocrat. She favors freedom of conscience and religion for everyone, including non-Christians. However, she also thinks that the moral teachings of Christianity are true. She perceives no incoherence or incompatibility between supporting the rights of other people to hold wrong views, on the one hand and advocating for views that she finds to be true. Moreover, she thinks that laws should teach true morals rather than falsehoods. Therefore, she supports legal reforms that are predominantly pro-life and pro-family.

MORALISTS FOR GOOD

One tendency that prevents us from achieving civil and reasoned discourse is that we misunderstand each other's motivations. We fail to respond to other people's stated concerns and ideals and instead attribute to them motivations they have not expressed and do not hold. Sometimes we do this because we are projecting onto the person in front of us a prior experience with some other person who advocated for the same or similar principles or proposals. But we should respect others enough to respond to their actual sentiments and arguments rather than force them to defend views they might not espouse.

Reese Cycler is not anti-business. He is not motivated to destroy other people's jobs but rather to steward the natural environment. It is fair game to point out the economic consequences of his preferred policy proposals. However, it is neither civil nor productive to attribute to him a desire or intention to bring about those consequences.

Lawson Order is neither a racist nor a xenophobe. He does not intend to discriminate against people based on their race. Nor does he want children to suffer needless injustices in their countries of origin. He wants to secure the rule of law and prosperity there as well as here. It is fair game to point out to him the human cost of immigration enforcement. However, to suppose that he wants or intends for migrants to suffer needlessly is both to miss his reasons and to treat him unjustly.

I. Denti Tarian is neither a snowflake nor a rabble-rouser. Her objective is not to silence speech she finds offensive. She wants to ensure that people are not rejected or ostracized because of their sexual orientation or gender identity. It is fair game to point out that redefining marriage and sex threatens the rights of children to be connected to their mother and father and to know their true nature. However, we should not assume that she intends that threat.

Dee Vine Leeledd is not a theocrat. She is not trying to establish a sectarian, religious government. She believes that the norms of conduct that Christianity teaches are objectively good for everyone, and she wants people to follow them to achieve genuine happiness. It is fair game to point out that not everyone agrees with her religious convictions and that giving them the force of law might burden the consciences of others. However, to accuse her of trying to force her religious beliefs on others is to misstate her motivations and to fail to appreciate what is universal in her moral beliefs.

Many people suspect that the motivations of moralists such as these are not sincere. They think that moral expressions are mere pretexts and that those who go about telling others about their moral obligations are really attempting to grab and consolidate power. They might say of our four moralists that they are trying to force their views on others. But notice that the moralists do you not view themselves that way. Each thinks that he or she knows how to make the world a better place, and the evidence of their sincerity is found in their actions. They act on their convictions. They have integrity.

Each of our moralists is acting on his or her understanding of what is good and right. And each is trying to accomplish whatever good he or she can. Reese believes that he is helping to save the planet and, thereby, enabling everyone to live longer, healthier, and more sustainable lives. Lawson believes that he is advocating for an orderly and just society in which everyone can enjoy equal opportunities within the rules laid down by lawful authorities. Denti believes that she is helping the marginalized to find love and acceptance. Dee Vine believes that she is sharing good news, revealing to others the path away from discontentment and cynicism and into joy and contentment.

To be sure, many power-hungry people use the rhetoric of moral obligation to gain and consolidate power, especially political power. Moral rhetoric activates a person's conscience and motivates them to want to do something right and avoid doing things that are wrong. That's what moral rhetoric is for. Ambitious people can cynically leverage this natural response in others for their own selfish ambitions. Cynics and hypocrites abound.

Our concern here is not the cynics and hypocrites but rather those who genuinely want to do what is right and want to have more productive discourse with their neighbors about what is right to do. Consider our four moralists as archetypes of sincere friends and neighbors whom you know, who genuinely believe that they have some knowledge about what is good and right, and who want to share that knowledge with others because they want their communities to be better off.

Our four moralists will not easily get along with each other. Each holds views that others find unacceptable, perhaps even abhorrent. Each looks for truth in authorities that others reject. These differences matter. But they should not prevent us from seeing what our four moralists have in common. Each wants to bring about some aspect of the common good for everyone. To understand this is to begin to make civil discourse possible.

NOTES

1. Ed Pilkington, "Obama Angers Midwest Voters with Guns and Religion Remark," *The Guardian* (April 14, 2008), https://www.theguardian.com/world/2008/apr/14/barackobama.uselections2008.

2. Peter Baker, "The Profanity President: Trump's Four-Letter Vocabulary," *New York Times* (May 19, 2019), https://www.nytimes.com/2019/05/19/us/politics/trump-language.html.

3. Ibid.

THREE

A Collection of Selfies

Our fractious moralism poses a challenge. Moreover, the demise of political neutrality unsettles many of us who have lived our lives enjoying civil liberties and the other fruits of a free and virtuous society. But the generation now in charge will pass from the stage, as all others have before them. Perhaps the next generation will reason better about controversial moral questions and will have less of an appetite for authoritarian control.

Unfortunately, the attitudes and sentiments of younger generations do not give us cause for optimism. The future does not look more liberal or tolerant, it just looks . . . different. To focus on the generation now coming of age is to confront a challenge that we have not yet fully understood.

A TRUTH FOR EACH

In recent years, several students have expressed opinions that go something like this:

1. I have my truth, and Aristotle has his truth.
2. My truth is equally as valid as Aristotle's truth.
3. Aristotle was a racist and sexist.
4. Therefore, Aristotle's truth is invalid.

This is nonsense. This argument is not merely a bad argument; it is no argument. It is incoherent. It either contradicts itself or entails the additional conclusion that "my truth" is equally as invalid as "Aristotle's truth," in which case none of us has reason to care what the speaker is saying.

The student making the argument presupposes that there is no objective truth, only two subjective opinions: the student's "truth" and Aristotle's "truth." This gives us no reason to prefer either opinion over the other, or even to care about them. In this sense, they are both equally valid and equally meaningless.

Alternatively, the student might presuppose that the validity of opinions is measured against some objective standard. But the student asserts that Aristotle's opinion is invalid and that the validity of Aristotle's opinion is equal to his own. That logically entails that the student's opinion is also invalid, and so we should reject the student's opinion that Aristotle's opinion is invalid.

Even though this argument offers nothing rational to believe, many students seem to believe it. Indeed, students today have many strong, moral opinions that mean nothing. They believe in right and wrong and justice. They have strong views about what should be believed and what should and should not be done. Their opinions are not often well-formed or articulated. They are not even always coherent. However, the students hold them dearly.

These students' opinions are their own and theirs alone. Their opinions do not refer to any propositions or ideals or practices—either permanent or cultural—that are out there to be discovered in the world. They offer us nothing intelligible to accept or reject. Instead, to the extent that they take any propositions or ideals on board, those raw materials are shaped to fit into their subjective identities. Everyone is his own tribe. Everyone has his own truth.

A few months ago, an article appeared on social media that illustrates this muddle. It might have been written as an anthem for the generation now coming of age. The article was titled, "This Canadian Fashion Brand Wants to Create Equality and Acceptance, One T-Shirt at a Time." It concerned an audio-visual advertisement campaign that flashes the smiling faces of different pairs of people across the screen. The soundtrack is a recitation of a poem, which expresses a preference for the word "and" over the word "or." It declaims that "we" are many things, including things that are generally understood to be different. We are both black and white; both pescatarian and eating a bacon-covered donut.

As a description of the pluralism that characterizes Western societies, this ad paints a colorful picture. But the advertisers make clear that their aspiration is not merely to describe. Their ambition is profoundly moral, even quasi-religious. The advertisement ends with a short creed: "We believe our differences are not obstacles to overcome. True inclusion—[sic] is coming together and celebrating the things that set us apart." The fashion company's CEO expressed his motivation for the ad campaign in similar terms. "In the end," he explained, "it's most important for our brand to celebrate inclusion on a global level highlighting the beauty of diversity, as one of humanity's greatest gifts."[1]

The advertisement is presumably effective; ad agencies don't spend significant resources on products in which they have no confidence. One would expect an ad to reflect the culture to which it is designed to appeal. And, indeed, the poem reflects how many young people today speak. Many of the students one encounters would not only react favorably to this ad, they would say that it expresses their truths.

This is challenging. As a creed—a statement of what we together believe—the ad is incoherent. There is no set of truths with which one could agree or disagree. To the extent that the ad expresses universal truths—general propositions—it contradicts itself. One cannot be a pescatarian *and* eat donuts with bacon. One cannot be "born like this" *and* be what one wears, as the poem insists.

Some of the sentiments expressed in the advertisement are not inherently contradictory, but they are so ambiguous that they seem meaningless. Assuming that diversity is "one of humanity's greatest gifts," is it a gift from someone *to* humanity or *from* humanity to someone? And who is the someone? If "true inclusion" is "coming together and celebrating the things that set us apart," are we not being inclusive if we all come together merely to play a baseball game or sing campfire songs? Moreover, if we celebrate the things that set us apart, then in what sense are we creating "equality"? To be "equal" means to be the same in some relevant respect. Equality is not inherently diverse. Indeed, it is usually the opponent of true diversity.

The ad might be understood as an expression of belief in diversity. However, then it is not a statement of what we *should* believe or affirm, only a descriptive statement that we are, as a matter of fact, different. Read that way, it is not even a statement about what *we* are. *Some* of us are Muslim, and *others* of us are Sikhs . . . and *others* are Christian, and *others* are Jews. But one cannot be all religions at once. *Some* of us are black, and *others* are white. However, if we all are both, then it cannot mean anything to be either.

The ad reflects an ancient human longing—to know who "we" are, to know what it means to be a human being. But the ad cannot provide a coherent account of who "we" are precisely because its stated purpose is to celebrate "the things that set us apart." It is not a creed about what unites us but rather an ode to what divides us into clans, groups, and associations. Any group of people whom we can identify as a group is identifiable precisely as a group who are some things and not others. To be Muslim is precisely *not* to be Christian. A symphony orchestra is a symphony orchestra insofar as it is not a jazz band or a football team. Groups that get together to eat donuts with bacon are . . . whatever they are partly insofar as they are not pescatarians. The ad celebrates a kind of tribalism.

Perhaps the one falsifiable truth claim in the entire poem is this one: "And we are absurd."

TRIBES OF ONE

But maybe not. One can understand the sentiment of this advertisement if one correctly understands what is meant by "we." Conversations with younger students lead one to conclude that they do not think of "us" and "we" as an identifiable group of people organized around common good or shared political ideals. "We" are not identified by shared principles that render all of our beliefs coherent and obligatory. Rather, "we" are just the set of people who happen to be here, whether here is this room, this social media feed, this profession, or on this Earth.

This is tribalism not of groups and associations but of atomized individuals. There is no association or group of pescatarians, only the set of individuals who choose (for now) to eat only fish. One is not Muslim because one belongs to an ancient and communal faith group constituted by established, immutable convictions and practices but because one happens to identify (for now) with the idea of being Muslim. This is why, for example, a young person today might call herself a Muslim or a Roman Catholic or a Baptist and, yet, personally reject some or even many of the teachings of the religion with which she identifies. She is not Muslim or Catholic by virtue of her adherence and conformity to the dogmas and practices of a faith tradition; the idea of the faith tradition is useful to her (for now). The truth claims of Sharia or the Catechism do not shape her convictions and identity. She shapes her own identity.

"We" turn out to be a collection of selfies, which are carefully crafted, externally projected images of individual self-constitution. The characteristics that used to constitute communities of people are now just useful materials from which one can choose to build one's own personalized identity, à la carte. No longer do individuals identify as members of the community by being part of the community, sharing its practices, and submitting to its norms. Instead, identification with the community is a product of individual choices to put on certain aspects of the community's brand.

Consider a hypothetical young person, Sammy Student. Though fictional, Sammy resembles most of the students one encounters in a university classroom today. Sammy identifies as Roman Catholic because he thinks of himself as spiritual, his parents are Catholic, and he is pescatarian, and Catholics eat fish on Fridays. However, he does not like the Catholic Church's teachings on sexuality and marriage, so he identifies as an LGBT-ally Catholic. And the Church is not as strongly in favor of economic liberties as he would prefer, so he also identifies as libertarian Catholic (but not a member of the Libertarian Party).

Georgia Graduate also identifies as Roman Catholic because she likes the idea of belonging to a tradition. But like Sammy, Georgia rejects some of the Church's teachings. She likes the Christian idea that human beings are created in the image of God. This idea suggests to her that humans are capable of excellence, even god-like greatness. But she objects to the dogma that all human beings have equal and inherent moral worth. She has read the writings of eugenicists Harry Hamilton Laughlin and Margaret Sanger. She is persuaded that some human lives are worthier than others. Some people are just not capable of greatness.

Sammy and Georgia have strong moral opinions. Unlike the teachings of the Church with which they identify, their opinions are not comprehensive and coherent. They have chosen for themselves opinions that contradict other opinions that they also claim to hold. Yet they hold and express their opinions with ardor and fervor. They are authentic to themselves.

EVERYTHING IS PERSONAL

Many of our students are trapped in their selfies. They often arrive in our classrooms, offices, shop floors, and religious assemblies with no appetite for the teachings of Aristotle or Moses, only for their own, individual "truths." To be sure, some of their truths are others-focused. But even the most altruistic of their personal motivations are not inherently oriented toward the good of others, only contingently so. If my truth is that I should give my money to the poor and join a religious order, then that's what I should do. If someone else's truth is that he should spend his money on prostitution, then, my students want to know, who are you to judge? Yet these same students do judge others.

In other words, our students are unwilling to do what it takes to equip themselves to know what is right to do. They are stuck in a "selfie stand-off."

The fundamental problem is that, on the whole, young people have made their moral reasoning thoroughly personal. When deciding what is right to do, they generally look to themselves for guidance. Their guiding principle is authenticity. What matters most to them—the only thing that matters to some of them—is that they are true to themselves.

This is a different and, in some ways, more profound challenge than the demise of political neutrality and the rise of moral reasoning. Two people with very different moral principles and substantive views might both be looking to the same sources for moral guidance but interpret those sources differently. For example, members of a religious tradition do not always agree about economic or immigration policies, but they nevertheless agree that religious sources of moral instruction—sacred texts, the general councils of their religious leaders, clergy, catechisms—should determine what is to be done. They disagree about the meaning of those sources, but they agree that the answer lies within the sources themselves rather than their own opinions about those sources. As a result, they can reason together, even if they do not ultimately agree.

By contrast, many young people think that their own opinions are what matter. They have no neutral ground on which to reason together because their sources of authority and guidance are not external to themselves. Each has her own truth. Their differences are not merely differences of judgment or interpretation. Their differences go all the way down to the source.

When one asks candid questions about these differences, one finds that they tend to be generational rather than ideological. When invited to explain their decision-making, members of the same generation tend to describe similar motivations while members of different generations describe quite different motivations, regardless of political or ideological tendencies. Nor can these differences be attributed to structural changes in society. When asked to identify the most important influences on their moral views, people of all generations identify parents, teachers, coaches, sacred texts, religious communities, and friends. Therefore, young people have learned moral reasoning from the same people and institutions as older people. But they learned something radically different.

Members of the so-called Silent Generation—those who came of age during World War II and who fought in the Korean conflict and the Cold War—tend to speak in terms of virtues and duties. They speak of "honor" and "speaking the truth." They learned these virtues from virtuous elders. As one member of this generation puts it, "My father, my grandfather, people I grew up with, just sort of modeled [those virtues] without preaching anything to me." And they learned the virtues from hearing and reading stories of virtuous people. They were steeped in classical and sacred texts about people who did the right thing in difficult circumstances. As a result, they do not experience internal conflict when doing the right thing entails undesirable consequences. Doing the right thing is just what one does. Accept the consequences, whatever comes.

For example, an older gentleman who served as a fighter pilot in the Cold War describes assignments that were obviously "suicide missions." The pilots simply "lived with that." They did what the mission required. They did not think "it was a big deal." One did what one's duty required. The question of whether to climb into the cockpit and fly the mission "wasn't even a moral conflict."

Some younger people today speak in similar terms, especially those trained in the military and those educated in monotheistic intellectual traditions, such as Judaism and Christian social thought. But in more recent generations, such people tend to stand out. Among those who came of age before the 1960s, sentiments of virtue and duty are ubiquitous.

Members of the so-called Generation X, who are now entering middle age, seem to trust their own judgment and virtue less than the Silent Generation. They are more motivated to take external consequences into account and tend to take their guidance from mission statements, group objectives, and rules. For example, a middle-aged military officer describes his training as "all about the mission." He describes a situation in which he had to make the difficult decision to report a subordinate for doing something that was "obviously wrong." The moral question was whether to report the subordinate or instead to "shut my mouth and play the team player." In persuading himself to make the report, which he "knew to be right," he "fell back on the UCMJ [Uniform Code of Military Justice]. That tells me what's right and wrong."

Similarly, a Gen-X-er who worked as a therapist had to decide what to think about a co-worker's conduct. When deciding what to do, she "wanted the rules." She wanted guidance that was clear. She "didn't want to be free-wheeling, just myself." For this person and others of her generation, doing the right thing is not automatic. But there is a formula. It consists of finding and interpreting the rules or the mission statement and then doing what they require.

Members of the so-called Millennial Generation, who are now on their way out of our college and university classrooms and moving to the working world, at first appear to have similar external motivations. When asked to say what they "generally think that people should do," they use words and phrases such as "good," "right," and "treat people how they want to be treated." When asked what "most people actually do," they use words and phrases such as "evil," "wrong," "bad," "a mix of good and bad," and "what is best for themselves." They express moral sentiments and judgments freely. However, scratch below the rhetoric and one finds not virtues or rules but rather feelings and personal identities. By "right" and "good," they tend to mean "what is right for me," or "what I find satisfying." By "wrong" and "bad," they tend to mean "what makes people feel bad."

These conversations reveal a critical divide in our moral discourse. Older members of our society tend to speak of moral motivations and criteria that they did not create. They speak of virtues displayed by their parents and mentors, duties that they owe to other people, fidelity to the mission of their unit or the success of the business in which they are employed. They look to rules and regulations governing the groups and communities of which they are part and the ways in which their choices and actions will affect the interests of other people. Their motivations are focused outward, and their criteria for making decisions are external to themselves.

By contrast, when explaining their moral reasoning, younger folks tend to refer to their own feelings, well-being, and opinions. Even when they draw on the terminology of religion or virtue or rights, they concentrate on the effects that such sources of guidance have on them. Their motivations and criteria are focused inward.

Even when members of different generations use the same words, they tend to mean different things. For example, the Generation X military officer talks about how difficult it was for him to discipline a younger subordinate for breaking the rules. He knows it was the right thing to do, but nevertheless, it was "painful." By using that word, he does not mean to suggest that the cost was merely emotional. Rather, he goes on to explain that the pain resulted from the break in his relationship with the subordinate, who would now be the subject of professional censure as a result.

This officer is speaking about his personal feelings. But the reference point for his feelings—the motivation that made his obedience to the rules difficult—is not *that* he felt bad, but rather *why* he felt bad. He paid attention to his feelings because his feelings motivated him to account for the motivations and well-being of someone else. His motivations are externally focused, even when he uses language about his own subjective, internal experience.

Conversely, a younger student describes an occasion when he did something unpopular because it was the "right thing to do." By using that phrase, he does not mean that his action was right in some objective sense, but rather that it was right *for him*. What he did was against the rules of his community, and it did not benefit anyone other than himself. Therefore, in what sense could it have been right? The student explains that the activity made him feel good about himself, and therefore, he believes he acted rightly.

This younger student, a member of the so-called Millennial Generation, is using language that earlier generations used to refer to objective standards of right and wrong. But he has an entirely different meaning. His reference point is not external to himself. In fact, he disregards the external considerations that counted against his decision—the views of other people, who perceived his conduct as selfish, and the rules that he was flouting. His point of reference in determining what is right is his own subjective, internal experience.

JUDGMENT

Young people do have one objective principle: They refuse to discriminate. They reject the practice of drawing distinctions, so they lack the ability to form judgments. Because they will not discriminate, they cannot distinguish between what is to be done and what is not to be done. They are allergic to discrimination. As a result, they are allergic to reason. They do not think very well because they reject on principled grounds the habits and practices on which right-thinking depends.

We need to think well to do what is right. To act well, we must first judge, and then we must decide. Therefore, the principled rejection of discrimination and judgment portends difficult practical challenges.

Insofar as humans are practical beings, we are naturally judgmental beings. Every moment, we act, and many moments, we *choose* to act or refrain from acting. Choosing and acting requires discernment (i.e., "this is this"), discrimination (i.e., "this is not that"), and judgment (i.e., "this is to be done, not that"). Judgment is not a bad thing. Nor is it an inherently good thing. It is merely a fact of life. It is a necessary thing.

Because we must judge, we should learn to judge well. Discernment, discrimination, and judgment can be better or worse, right or wrong. And because bad judgment often has bad consequences, people generally have natural incentives to judge rightly and correctly. We cannot avoid judgment. By refusing to reason to judgment, we only avoid making *sound* judgments.

A great irony of our age is that young people condemn those whom they deem to be judgmental. The sidewalk evangelist or country preacher is held up for disapproval alongside the swindler and the crooked politician. Many actions that previous generations deemed wrong are now accepted, even celebrated, while the act of deeming something wrong is condemned as intolerant or bigoted. Our young people are judgmental of those who exercise judgment. No "-ism" is more judgmental than nonjudgmentalism.

Those who come in for the most emphatic condemnation—the harshest judgment—are often those who appeal to objective standards of reason, such as conscience, human nature, and divine law. Therefore, the irony of the nonjudgmental posture is really a double irony. Young people express judgment of those who appeal to standards of right judgment. Implicit in this condemnation is that the actions of judgmental people fail to conform to some objective standard of right judgment. But our young people have no coherent account of what that objective standard is.

THE POLITICS OF THE PERSONAL

One result of this confusion is personal isolation. Sammy Student and Georgia Graduate have lots to say. But they do not have anything meaningful to say to each other. Each of them projects an inward identity out toward the world. Each identity is constituted in large part by beliefs. However, neither of them is capable of engaging the merits of the others' beliefs. Sammy cannot evaluate the beliefs of Georgia as being either true or false beliefs, only as being authentically *Georgia's* beliefs. Likewise, Georgia has no basis for accepting or rejecting Sammy's convictions for herself. She has no reason to think that Sammy's opinions are worthy of acceptance by anyone other than Sammy. She can only accept that Sammy holds them.

Sammy and Georgia hold beliefs inside themselves. Those beliefs do not correspond to any truths outside themselves. They do not rise to the level of knowledge. Georgia likes the Christian idea that humans are god-like, and her affection for that idea and acceptance of it as her own personal truth makes it true for her. She would not dare to presume that it is also true for Sammy or for anyone else.

Nevertheless, Sammy and Georgia both hold their beliefs as essential aspects of their identities. So, the stakes are very high. For anyone not to accept their beliefs is for that person to reject *them*, Sammy and Georgia, as persons. Their beliefs and opinions could not be more personal. For someone not to accept the authenticity or validity of their beliefs is for that someone to jeopardize their identities as persons. It is, in contemporary parlance, so common now among young people, to "erase" them.

Now notice what happens when Sammy or Georgia meets one of the moralists we encountered in Chapter 2. Those folks hold that their convictions are true, not just for themselves but for everyone. They understand their convictions to be objectively and universally true. For example, Dee Vine Leeledd believes that all human beings are, in fact, created in the image of God and are bearers of equal and intrinsic worth and dignity, regardless of their virtues and achievements. Dee will, therefore, reject as false Georgia's expressed belief that some people who are not capable of greatness live unworthy lives. Dee will insist that Georgia's belief is false not only for Dee but also for Georgia. Georgia, she will insist, is wrong.

And here comes the crisis. From Georgia's perspective, her belief is at the core of who Georgia is. It is an essential aspect of her personal identity, her existence as a self-constituted and unique individual person. For Dee to reject Georgia's belief is, from Georgia's perspective, to cause an important aspect of Georgia to cease to be. From Georgia's perspective, the real Georgia who resides within her body and expresses itself as a moral agent seeking existence out there in the world has been denied the equal right to have acceptance and dignity. She has suffered what some people today call "dignitary harm."

Now, a question of immense importance to many people has become inextricably personal to Georgia. She cannot dispassionately and rationally evaluate the arguments for and against her opinion because at stake is the very existence of an essential part of her identity. She *cannot afford to be wrong*—her opinion cannot be rejected as false—or else an essential part of her ceases to be.

Multiply this example by millions of young people, and it becomes apparent that the crisis of our fractured discourse will only get worse. As personal and no-holds-barred as our public discourse is at present, wait until it is being conducted largely by young people who believe that every political disagreement is moral, and that their very existence is at stake in every moral disagreement.

LOOKING BACKWARD TO MOVE FORWARD

What do we do now? We can start by looking backward. To render judgments that are good, we need to judge well. We need reason. And we need wisdom. By reflecting on the judgments and practical reasons that human beings have proposed throughout the millennia of recorded human history, we can begin to see the desirability of wisdom. But to understand those sources of wisdom, we must understand the meanings of the words they used.

The challenge before us is how to pursue knowledge well. Knowledge consists of beliefs that correspond to reality and which are, therefore, true. And here again, we are stuck. We cannot seem to agree on moral truth. Moreover, as we have already seen, we cannot agree for two reasons. First, we disagree about the values and principles at stake. In many cases, our values and principles are in direct and irreconcilable conflict. Second, we disagree about where to look for moral truth, whether it is in virtue or rules or religious convictions or personal identity. It seems that our inquiry about what is right to do is once again immobilized.

If we are to get unstuck, then we need help from those who are standing on solid ground. Or at the very least, we need to reach out to those who are on different ground. We cannot break free by struggling more furiously in the same mire. That we distrust each other and find moral failings in each other suggests that we might have to look outside our own age for guidance. We cannot look to the future, of course. However, we can look to the past.

We might look for help at Aristotle, Moses, Mary, the mother of Jesus, and Saint Teresa of Calcutta. Those men and women delivered to us the intellectual resources with which to discriminate between just and unjust actions, good and bad, right and wrong. We know what ethical failings *are* because Aristotle and Moses taught us. We know what is good and admirable to do because Saint Mary and Mother Teresa showed us.

That is an abstract statement. To make it particular, let us begin closer to home. We all have inherited gifts from those who lived before us. Therefore, each of us can identify something that should make us grateful to those who preceded us on Earth, no matter how flawed they were.

My family lives in what is known as an urban forest in a Southern city. Our neighborhood is a historic district that prides itself on having preserved its old houses, no matter how outdated those houses now seem, and its ancient trees, though those trees often prove inconvenient. As a result, in the sweltering heat and paved commercialization of twenty-first-century Dixie, our neighborhood is an oasis of shade and beauty.

Among the trees on our premises stand four mature oaks. Two of them shed in the late autumn and early winter. The other two are live oaks, which dispense their leaves in the spring. It seems that we spend most of the year raking leaves. When laboring at that task, it is easy to forget how much shade the trees cast on our house, how they keep our electricity bills low, and how our children delight in climbing them and playing under them. The work is not always pleasant, and it is almost always inconvenient. It is easy to forget the benefits of the trees when bearing the burdens of the trees.

It is even easier to forget that we would not enjoy the benefits of those trees had someone not had the foresight to cultivate and preserve them on occasions when it would have been easier and cheaper to cut them down, to make way for construction equipment and other modern conveniences. The existence of these trees in our yard was not inevitable. The trees are a gift from people who owned this house before we did, people whom we will never meet, and who do not now enjoy their shade.

Those people could not have preserved the trees had they not had the legal right to prevent other people from injuring or destroying the trees. Therefore, we owe our trees also to those who preserved the norms and institutions of property ownership that the State of Alabama inherited centuries ago from Great Britain. We also owe a debt to those who have enforced the laws.

We can scale this up. What is true of the mature trees in our neighborhood is also true of the institutions that employ us and the professional and vocational knowledge that we learn, practice, and impart in them. It is true of the religious assemblies where we worship and the liturgies we recite. It is true of the schools that our children attend and the subjects they learn, the concerts and games we attend, the theaters and gymnasiums and other institutions in which we participate, and most of the other cultural artifacts and growths that have been passed to us.

Now scale this up one more time: Why is there such a thing as law at all? Many, many people throughout history—perhaps most of those who have lived—have not had the benefit of the rule of law. They have lived instead either in anarchy and jeopardy of life and possessions or under tyranny and arbitrary rule. Those of us who live in countries that have the rule of law are very fortunate to enjoy this cultural heritage. The rule of law was not inevitable. Those who came before us had to invent it and fight hard to secure it.

It was not inevitable that Hammurabi should promulgate his Code, or that Moses should bring the Ten Commandments down from Mount Sinai, or that Justinian should compile his *Corpus Juris Civilis*, or that King John should be forced to sign Magna Carta, or that William Blackstone should write his *Commentaries on the Laws of England*, or that Joseph Story should design a common-law curriculum at Harvard University. And without those great human achievements, and without their continued maintenance and passage down from one generation to the next, it is doubtful that we would have lived in a time and place of ordered liberty.

Similarly, why is there such a thing as philosophy, or science, or music? These are gifts, which others created or purchased at the cost of immense personal sacrifice. Without their achievements, we might not have the civilization we enjoy today. We remember this too seldom. Gratitude toward those who came before us does not come naturally to us. We must actively cultivate it in ourselves by learning and relearning the origins and foundations of these gifts. If we do not do this, then our understanding will be impoverished, bereft of the full benefits we enjoy from institutions and practices that we inherited from others.

Some months ago, a respondent to an essay of mine proved this point. The essay explained, in part, why law professors should require law students to read classic texts such as Aristotle's *Ethics*. In the comment section below the essay, one critic pointedly wrote, "Fahk [sic] Aristotle . . . he was a Pedophile." In the commenter's judgment, we can safely disregard Aristotle's teachings about logic, virtue, justice, and the rest because Aristotle and his fellow ancient Greeks tolerated pedophilia.

The judgment of this commenter rests on (at least) two implicit judgments: First, that Aristotle's (alleged) pedophilia was morally wrong, and second, that we, therefore, can safely disregard what Aristotle taught. The first judgment is surely correct, but how do we know that? The only way for us to render reasoned judgment about the sexual conduct of ancient Greeks is to employ the very intellectual resources—logic and reasoned analysis, insights about virtue, vice, and human action—that the commenter's second judgment dismisses as unworthy.

For one thing, how do we even know what a pedophile is? The words "pedo" and "philia" are Greek. In condemning the Greeks as pedophiles, we employ a language that the Greeks gave us. If we are to disregard all they said, then we should use words of our own invention.

For another thing, we have no reason to take the commenter's judgment seriously and judge accordingly unless he has a reasoned basis for his judgment. However, it is impossible to render a reasoned judgment about ancient Greek sexual practices without employing the philosophical tools the ancient Greeks discovered and honed. How would we and Aristotle know that he *should* not engage in pedophilia unless there is some objective standard to which his reason and our reason can both refer and that we can all understand? Would we have known how to think and speak of that standard had Aristotle and his teachers not given us the ideas of justice and injustice? Moreover, how would we know how to reason together about justice had Aristotle not taught us logic? Try making a reasoned argument about the immorality of pedophilia without making reference to justice, using logic, or articulating propositions about what is good for humans to do.

The commenter's second judgment—that because Aristotle engaged in morally culpable behavior, we can safely dismiss all of his teachings—undermines the force of his first judgment that Aristotle's putative conduct was morally culpable. Aristotle's teachings include the tools necessary to render a rational judgment about the moral culpability of Aristotle's conduct, especially logic and knowledge of the virtues. The commenter did not successfully show that we should not bother to read and understand Aristotle. On the contrary, the commenter showed that he does not understand Aristotle and that he is foolish.

THE DEBT WE OWE TO OTHERS

We can generalize this lesson: None of us is born speaking in complete sentences and exercising right judgment. We must be taught by those who are willing to set aside their own satisfaction and to invest in helping us to mature into speaking, reasoning agents. We owe to other people our very ability to reason and speak about what is to be done.

Those who invest knowledge in us received it from someone else. Apart from the rare William Shakespeare or J. R. R. Tolkien, almost none of us are capable of creating a language to express the complexity of human experience. Even Shakespeare and Tolkien borrowed heavily from others. And as for a Socrates or an Aristotle—one who can reflect so critically and insightfully and persistently about the nature of reflection as to make philosophy possible—all of recorded human history has produced only a handful of them. Nearly everyone else received their language and logic from others.

Even if one thinks that self-constituted, personal identity is what matters most, one can see that one's personal identity is not *entirely* self-constituted. One could not know, much less express, one's personal truth without using language received as an inheritance. One could not constitute one's identity as a lawyer unless someone had built and sustained institutions of legal education and practice. Sammy Student and Georgia Graduate could not identify as Roman Catholic were there not a Roman Catholic Church and those willing to preserve it. The objects and means of pursuit that people employ to become their true "selves" all came from someone else.

Knowledge of self, like knowledge of the world, is expressed and acquired in the community. The pursuit of that knowledge requires cooperation with the communities of which we are now part—this class of students, this university, this academic discipline, this political community. And those communities were built by those who came before us. Bradley C. S. Watson observes that the Delphic admonition to know thyself has been taken up throughout history with fruitful effects where the self is understood *in community*. "[S]ome of the greatest works in the Western tradition concern their authors' own education, or the education of the great men on whom the authors dilate. But knowledge of the self cannot help but be a reflection on the self's relation to the outside world, including especially the civic world."[2]

We have reason to be grateful for the communities that we have inherited from others, for they make our understanding possible. They even make it possible to understand ourselves.

GRATITUDE

We all have far more cause to be grateful than we care to acknowledge. We exist because of the actions of others (or perhaps, as most religions teach, the Other). We also have inherited a rich heritage of language, logic, wisdom, custom, tradition, and cultural institutions, none of which we built. We inhabit a civilization that others built for us and bequeathed to us, men and women who expected nothing in return from us. We do not reflect on this often enough. We tend to overemphasize the merits of our own contributions to the world and, when we reflect on them at all, to minimize the contributions and emphasize the failures of those who lived before us.

Reflecting on the contributions of those who came before us is a way of expressing gratitude to them. Gratitude is an important virtue because it opens us to receive gifts and treasures from others. It frees us from having to create our identity and values from scratch all by ourselves. It enables us to participate in celebrating a common good and to help cultivate it for those to come.

This reflection also benefits us regarding our identity. We benefit not only from reflecting on our inheritances and our debts to others but also from examining the names borne upon the practices and institutions that we have inherited, so that we can know better who we are.

- A philosopher's identity is found in the practice of reasoning that descends from Socrates and Aristotle and Elizabeth Anscombe.
- A lawyer becomes a lawyer by doing well what Justinian, William Blackstone, Joseph Story, and Sandra Day O'Connor did before, even if we now do it in different ways and with respect to innovations and subject matters that they did not imagine.
- Scientists benefit from remembering not only the ideas of Aristotle, Isaac Newton, and Albert Einstein but who they were as people and how they lived their lives.
- Musicians might not want to emulate Wolfgang Amadeus Mozart or Miles Davis in all respects, but they would do well to consider what those men did well to cultivate and liberate their natural genius.

If we are to think and communicate well, we must be willing to consider the teachings and achievements of those who came before us. And we must do this even if we care only about our own individual identities.

After all, what really makes a selfie interesting is what lies in the background.

NOTES

1. Katie Richards, "This Canadian Fashion Brand Wants to Create Equality and Acceptance, One T-Shirt at a Time: Frank and Oak Celebrates Diversity with a Touching Film," Adweek.com (December 4, 2017), available at http://www.adweek.com/brand-marketing/this-canadian-fashion-brand-wants-to-create-equality-and-acceptance-one-t-shirt-at-a-time/.

2. Bradley C. S. Watson, "Just as the Twig Is Bent: Civic Education in an Age of Doubt," in *Civic Education and Culture*, Bradley C. S. Watson, ed. (Wilmington, DE: ISI Books 2005), xv.

FOUR

The Practical Question

Each of the public figures discussed in Chapter 1, every one of the four moralists discussed in Chapter 2, and each of the members of different generations discussed in Chapter 3 is offering an answer to a question that is not abstract and theoretical but concrete and urgent. They all either want to know or are offering answers to a common question: "What shall I do?" We cannot avoid this question, for we are beings who act and who can choose to act using our reason. In every moment of every day of our lives, we must decide, and we can deliberate before making our decisions.

Unless we are to choose and act blindly—without regard for what is right and good to do, and without regard to the most effective and just means to achieve our ends—we must have an answer to the question of what to do. We cannot avoid it. Indeed, we *desire* an answer. We want to know what we should and should not do. Our profound disagreements show that, as a society, we are confused. We cannot agree on where to look for guidance. Yet even our disagreements reveal a deeper agreement that something must be done about our problems, and that we should reason together about what to do.

Consider again the commenter who wants to dismiss all of Aristotle's teachings because Aristotle was a pedophile (discussed in Chapter 3). This comment is worth considering, for it succinctly expresses both the urge to render moral judgment and the moral and intellectual confusion that so pervade our discourse today. Yet it also reveals a way forward.

The comment reveals profound ignorance, not to mention ingratitude. It was Aristotle who identified for us the tools with which to render correct, reasoned judgment. Aristotle (and his predecessors Socrates and

Plato) showed us how to use the tools of logic and the language of virtue and vice. As we observed in Chapter 2, everyone has the capacity to deliberate and to render reasoned judgment, but not everyone develops the ability to do so well, with precision and accuracy—that is, with excellence. Aristotle taught us how to use the tools of reason to make and critique practical judgments, answers to the question of what I should do. These are the very tools that the commenter wants to employ to dismiss Aristotle.

The comment also reveals the commenter's own pride and his blindness to his own folly. He is willing to dismiss wise, time-tested teachings because the teacher is morally flawed, which is to say because the teacher is a human being. Does the commenter really think himself free of all flaws? If so, then he needs to know himself better. If not, then why should we care about his judgment that Aristotle was morally deficient?

It is difficult to reason well about what should be done when we casually dismiss as unworthy of consideration the best exemplars of logic and reason, including even the fathers of moral philosophy, who showed us how to use logical analysis. However, even in this commenter's dogma, one finds solid ground on which to build. This comment reflects simultaneous intellectual blindness and moral clarity. The commenter rightly judged that pedophilia is a wrong action and that the willingness of ancient Greeks to engage in that conduct reflects a certain corruption of their character, which has some bearing on the merits of their teachings.

For all the profound ingratitude that it reflects, the comment contains a kernel of wisdom. The commenter judged Aristotle's *words* on the basis of Aristotle's *actions*. The insight at work here is that our actions reveal something important about our understanding and about the worth of our judgments. Of course, that insight also comes from Aristotle.

Aristotle taught that we are what we do. A being is, in a sense, defined by its pursuits, the ends toward which it acts. A bird dog is an animal that points at or flushes out birds. A musician is a person who pursues excellent performance of music. It follows that we can assess the nature and character of a person by the purposes for which the person acts.

Later thinkers, such as Saint Paul, Gregory the Great, and Thomas Aquinas, built upon this teaching. They showed that people can *choose* to act for some purposes and not for others. Human beings can discern what is good and right to do—eat this apple, feed my children, help this old man whose car has broken down—and what is bad and wrong to do—smoke this cigarette, gamble away my earnings, splash mud on the stranded old man while driving by. We can deliberate about what purposes and actions are right and which are wrong, and we can set our wills on one or the other. We can choose to act well and rightly or badly and wrongly.

From these insights, we can begin to recover learning. We begin with a simple question. It is the same question that our four moralists are trying to answer.

What shall I do?

This question is the beginning of wisdom—in our age and in all ages. The question demands an answer, for each of us is always acting or refraining from acting in some way or another. And the act of asking this question demonstrates the importance of getting the answer right. We inquire because we think there are better and worse options, plans of action that are desirable and plans of action than are less-than-desirable, or undesirable, or even wrong.

In short, the question presupposes the existence and desirability of practical knowledge. Call it the "Practical Question."

The question is practical in that it addresses a real need—the need to act or refrain from acting, which presses on human beings at every waking moment of our lives. We often ask ourselves mundane versions of the Practical Question without being aware that we are doing it. We think about what time to set the alarm to wake us in the morning, and we wonder what meal to serve our family for breakfast and which route is best to drive to work. We are more aware of asking versions of the Practical Question when the stakes are more consequential. We ask ourselves where to enroll for trade school or college, which apartment to lease or which house to buy, and where to send our children for school.

In all of these practical inquiries, whether mundane or profound, real human goods are at stake—goods such as knowledge, health, and friendship. We often take those goods for granted. We seldom step back and reflect on *why* we want to get to work on time or receive an education or live near a city park or so on.

Nor do we ask and answer the Practical Question correctly as often as we should. We often ask the Practical Question of ourselves, but not always. And we do not always answer it well. We are always acting or refraining from acting. One cannot avoid doing. Doing is what human beings do. However, one can avoid deliberating and reasoning about our doing. As we all know, we often act without thinking.

Even more rarely do we study or examine the answers to the Practical Question that great thinkers and doers have offered in the past. The writings of people such as Aristotle and the actions of heroic figures such as Mother Teresa of Calcutta contain considerable wisdom about what is good and right to do. The Practical Question is an enduring question. People have been asking it as long as there have been people.

Many great and admirable people have thought well about answers to the Practical Question, including versions of it that are quite similar to the questions we ask today. They have answered mundane questions such as what to eat and when to take a nap. And they have answered profound questions such as whether we should more greatly value life or personal autonomy (a question underlying debates about assisted suicide), when should nations be willing to go to war (a question that political leaders should consider *before* assuming office), and whom should we recognize as members of our political communities (a question at the heart of our immigration debates). We can learn from their actions and their answers, even the erroneous ones.

THE PROMISE OF THE PRACTICAL QUESTION

The Practical Question has both practical and abstract aspects.[1] Merely asking it directs us to act reasonably. That makes it different from theoretical questions, such as, "Is there a God?"; speculative questions, such as, "What would have happened had the South won the Civil War?"; and trivial questions, such as, "Who won the National League batting title in 1987?" And it is different from purely theoretical questions in a way that matters to us. Our Practical Question demands an answer now so that we can act well and rightly both now and in the future.

One can often get away with answering purely theoretical, speculative, or trivial questions badly for a long time. Sometimes the answers don't really matter at all. If I go wrong in a trivial or *purely* speculative inquiry, my life is not appreciably less worse off. If I come to the conclusion that the United States Constitution was ratified in 1890, or that a water molecule is comprised of four atoms, I will be no less wrong than if I conclude that the beef sitting in the back of the refrigerator for the last three months is not rancid. But I will be less sick.

The Practical Question is not merely a matter of intellectual curiosity. The stakes are not always higher in practical inquiry than in theoretical inquiry, but they are often more immediate. This is one reason for scientists to test hypotheses on which engineers will rely. It is one thing for Einstein to posit the theory of general relativity and for students of physics to express skepticism. It is quite another to remain skeptical of Einstein's theory when sending a spaceship to Mars.

Asking the Practical Question can help us reason together more productively and with greater civility about our controversies. Consider controversies about immigration. As long as we stay at the level of abstract or theoretical reason, it is easy for us to remain mired in unproductive controversy and personal attacks. Some people on one side of the debate insist that the right to immigrate is a fundamental human right and that anyone who supports immigration enforcement lacks sympathy and concern for refugees and the least well-off. Some people on the other side of the debate insist that failure to enforce our immigration laws to the letter is a threat to our national security and that those who propose amnesty are trying to undermine the rule of law. From here, matters become heated and personal quickly.

If we reframe the immigration debate in practical terms, then we can remove acrimonious accusations about personal motivations, and we can focus on what is actually at stake. Consider the issue as a practical question about which persons should be admitted to our country. Person A is a refugee who suffered religious persecution in his home country. He adheres to a historically peaceful religion, such as Hinduism or Judaism, and has a healthy, intact family. He is well-educated and skilled in a useful trade. Person B is a convicted criminal with known terrorist sympathies and no established family commitments. Now put the question of whether we should admit or exclude these persons.

By comparing these (hypothetical) applicants for asylum or admission, we expose the implausibility of some of the more extreme, abstract claims that people assert in debates about immigration. The Practical Question what to do about Person B puts to rest the idea that anyone can rationally argue for completely open borders. And it shows that people who advocate for enforcement of immigration laws are not necessarily motivated by hate or bigotry but rather have legitimate concerns. The Practical Question what to do about Person A challenges the idea that we should enforce the textual, formal requirements of our immigration laws strictly and aggressively, without regard to the merits of applicants. Moreover, it shows that people who advocate for selective enforcement of immigration laws are not necessarily trying to undermine the rule of law but instead have legitimate concerns about how we enforce our laws and whether we will be a welcoming people.

Now we can generalize from the cases of Persons A and B. Having begun with a practical inquiry, we can now move up to a more abstract discussion about the general characteristics of desirable immigrants and undesirable immigrants. Of course, these cases are easy cases. We will find that most cases are less clear. And we will find that we must take into account other considerations, such as the capacity of our job market to absorb new laborers, the ability of our government and civic institutions to impart to immigrants a love of liberty and equality and to assimilate them into American culture, and much else. But once the discussion is proceeding along these lines, though it is challenging, it is the kind of discussion we need to have about an issue as complicated as immigration enforcement. And it no longer tends toward the viciously personal.

PRACTICAL, NOT MERELY PRAGMATIC

The Practical Question is not merely a pragmatic question. It does not concern only efficiency or effectiveness. It primarily concerns us—who we are and what is good and right for us to do. This is an enduring concern. The question "What should I do?" has been around as long as human beings because human beings have always wondered at our capacity for greatness, good, and evil.

We should not assume that our moment in history is entirely unique. Our disagreements can be misleading, even disorienting. In the present, things that were taken for granted until quite recently are now denied. And we are uncertain about the future. Our lives are changing, and this change seems both constant and more rapid than ever. The change is not only in our technologies, our culture, and our other external circumstances. It is also in us. *We* are changing. It is not apparent what sort of people we will be when this period of rapid change is over. But human history is full of change. Humans always have been prompted to ask where they were headed and what kind of people they would be when they got there.

What the future holds for us depends in large part on what kind of people we will be and what sort of society we will constitute for ourselves. Today we—Westerners, generally, and Americans, in particular— largely enjoy the fruits of a free and equal, creative, energetic, diligent, and prosperous society. We will continue to enjoy those fruits only if we constitute ourselves as a free and equal, creative, energetic, diligent, and prosperous people. That, in turn, depends upon how we educate ourselves. We cannot continue to enjoy the fruits of free and equal participation in a prosperous society if we do not learn to reason together about what is good and right.

The prospects at present are not promising. Consider a barely hypothetical case. The following image is a composite of many of the students who enter my first-year law school courses each fall. Like the commenter who wants to disregard Aristotle, this example portends significant challenges.

Picture someone who wants to achieve something. Imagine that he wants to become a philosopher or a lawyer or a scientist or a musician. Now imagine that he does not want to know anything about the history and concepts of his chosen profession. "Just teach me the rules" or "the scientific method" or "the scales," he insists. "Don't make me read about Aristotle" or Blackstone or Newton or Mozart.

Our student *says* that he wants a practical education and nothing more. However, what he really wants is a *pragmatic* education, not an education that is fully practical. He wants to acquire the skills necessary to pursue his craft competently, and he wants to receive the credentials that prove to the world that he has mastered those basic skills. Anything more would be of no use to him. Indeed, he is concerned about the future, not the past. He is concerned about making change and bringing about progress, not learning about obsolete ideas and traditions from superstitious and bigoted dead men.

You might find this student's attitude surprising. After all, what could be more practical and more useful than a thorough understanding of the people, customs, and ideas that have shaped the profession he seeks to enter? What could be more useful than to learn from the triumphs and failures of those who have come before us? What could be more imperative than to consider the struggles and challenges that others have overcome to bring about the free and flourishing society in which we live, and to consider why some societies are neither free nor prosperous? You might think that a truly practical education would include all of those elements.

Yet consider the case in more detail. This student is convinced that he will find fulfillment in making his dreams come true. This goal does not require him to reflect on the choices and achievements of others or to acquire the practical wisdom of others, especially of those who lived in the past. He believes that they could not hope to understand the opportunities of the present and future. No, he believes that he has everything he needs within himself except for the skills and credentials that you, the teacher, can bestow upon him. To find his objectives, he need only look to himself, to his own feelings and desires. He simply needs the courage to be true to what he finds within himself and the data and strategies that will help him achieve his goals.

This student is trapped in a prison of the self. His truth is the only truth. He is capable of reasoning and is able to reason in a limited sense. But he only wants reason that has instrumental utility in helping achieve his desired goals. He has no interest in reasoning about the value of those goals, whether they are good or not. He does not reason about any truths that are external to his own feelings except insofar as reason enables him to affirm and gratify those feelings. The problem is not that he cannot reason *effectively*. The problem is that he will not reason *about what ultimately matters*.

Our new student is neither particularly religious nor especially secular. Some of the students who think this way deny that there are any gods or uncaused "Cause." Others claim a particular God as the source of the blessings that they intend to claim and the dreams they intend to pursue. But few of them perceive any special obligation to any source of objective meaning, whether a god or evolutionary progress or a community of faith or their parents. Whether he is endowed with his desires by God, or the cosmos, or his selfish genes, our new student is confident that he will be happy when those desires are satisfied, whatever those desires happen to be.

THE LIMITATIONS OF FEELINGS

This archetype has been around a while. Our new student is not entirely new, and many gifted authors have turned their pens and tapped their keyboards over the last several decades documenting the decline of moral and civic education and connecting it to a prevailing selfishness.[2] However, a general sense prevails that things have gotten worse recently and that the rate of deterioration is accelerating.

In 1943, C. S. Lewis described how modern educational innovators were producing "Men without Chests," whose appetites of the belly are liberated from the governance of the head, and whose *feelings* govern the person without the direction of practical reason.[3] The innovators' project was to debunk moral truths and show them to be mere sentiments. They taught that all moral claims are on par with the feelings of students. According to the educational innovators, ideas such as "Greater love hath no man than that he lay down his life for his friends" and "Society ought to be preserved" do not express any judgments of reason. They do not rest in real, objective goods. They merely reflect the feelings or instincts of the speaker.[4]

This leaves students with a moral compass whose only reference points are fleeting feelings, which ebb and flow and change direction without warning and which are not oriented toward true north, what is right to do. The products of the educational innovations of the twentieth century are human beings whose emotions are not trained and ordered into stable sentiments directed toward the common good. Lewis foresaw that youths educated in the ways of skepticism about objective standards of right and wrong would come to believe "that all sentences containing a predicate of value are statements about the emotional state of the speaker."[5] He accurately predicted that students would, eventually, come to read all statements about morality as declarations about the emotions or subjective experience of the speaker, as most students do today. Feelings are the boss. This is an easy sell to young people who have, as the kids say, "all the feels."

This raises practical problems. Lewis observed that we see the problems most clearly when a civilization is threatened. Building and preserving what is valuable often requires great sacrifices. Sometimes the sacrifices required are total. When an existential threat appears, such as invasion by a totalitarian enemy, the survival of civilization requires that some people be willing to risk their lives in its defense. Moreover, we cannot employ reason to persuade any youth to sacrifice himself who has been educated in the feeling-based program of the innovators.

On the innovators' view, a choice to risk one's life to preserve one's community is no more rational and *no less* rational than a choice not to place oneself in harm's way. And students trained in the innovators' program have a moral compass that does not point north, toward the good. Instead, their compass needles wander all around, first to this feeling, and then to that one. We can offer these youths no reason to sacrifice themselves for others that they will accept because reason does not bear upon their ultimate choices.[6]

Lewis was looking to the future, predicting what would naturally result from the innovators' educational project. He wrote these words even as hundreds of thousands of the youths of the English-speaking world—Britain and her former colonies—who had been educated on the old model of practical reason were fighting and dying to defend Western civilization against tyranny around the world. Our elite educational institutions no longer provide an education that motivates young people to serve their country in war or to sacrifice themselves for others.[7] Our nation still produces young people who are willing to sacrifice. Many of them willingly go to war and perform heroic acts. However, the kind of education that we value most, on which we place the highest premium, has become a different kind of education. It teaches young people how to pursue their personal dreams but neglects to teach them about what is ultimately good.

Something has changed in our character as a people. In 1865, near the end of the campaign that would finally bring about Union victory in the American Civil War, the Union's Army of the Potomac encountered Confederate General Robert E. Lee's Army of Northern Virginia entrenched in elevated positions at Cold Harbor, near Mechanicsville, Virginia. The men who met in the battle that ensued were from all walks of life. And they shared a common set of assumptions about being willing to sacrifice oneself for a greater good.

Ken Burns's documentary about the Civil War explains that, as they prepared to charge Confederate trenches at Cold Harbor, Union soldiers sewed their names and hometowns on the backs of their coats. Union veterans of earlier battles, especially Fredericksburg and Spotsylvania, knew well how much mutilation and death would result from charging an entrenched position. They wanted to be identified to loved ones, and they knew that they might be unrecognizable without their names sewn on their backs. Yet knowing the carnage that awaited them, they put on their coats, lined up, and followed orders to attack.

In short, these men put aside their feelings of fear and dread and did what they understood to be right. This way of thinking is almost incomprehensible to many people today. Yet it persisted in our national character until quite recently. Those who served on the front lines in the first and second World Wars, nearly a century after the Civil War, spoke of running toward death and carnage in the same way that most of us think of going to our places of employment each weekday. "We were just doing our jobs," they would say. Our student who wants a pragmatic education to pursue his dreams does not reason this way. Indeed, it is doubtful that he can understand the reasoning of those earlier men, or even the war veterans in his midst.

We have changed. We elevate feelings at the expense of duty, so we wonder at the war heroes among us. They are unusual and extraordinary. Many of us no longer take it for granted that any one of us might be called upon to sacrifice himself for the good of the rest. And education is not unimportant or irrelevant to this change. Lewis was on to *something*.

THE PRACTICAL QUESTION IN EDUCATION

If we are to teach and learn, then we must have some practical question to motivate our efforts. Students will learn best who understand the *point* of learning. But even practical education often fails to be *fully* practical. Much of our education today is practical only in the thin, pragmatic sense. We teach and learn techniques and skills. We are not often engaged in the thick, mind- and soul-shaping enterprise of asking what is to be done in a comprehensive sense, with reference to what is good for us all.

Many educational innovators today have a thinned-out version of a practical question, much like our student who wants only a certain skill set and a credential. They ask, "How can I do this?" where *this* is some predetermined goal. Sometimes the goal is stated broadly as, for example, social justice, technological progress, or national defense. Sometimes it is stated more particularly as increased access to health care, reduced unemployment, more widespread Internet access, or defeating our enemies.

This thin version of a practical question is purely instrumental. It is not useless. However, while it is helpful to consider critically how to achieve our goals effectively and efficiently, that thin version of a practical education does not liberate us from the little prisons of self. It excludes from consideration the really important question of whether what we want to do is worth doing. It does not motivate us to consider good and bad, right and wrong.

This instrumental approach to inquiry and education can be quite dangerous. If our goals turn out to be bad or evil, or even if they turn out to be simply less-than-ideal, then to equip ourselves and our students to pursue those goals more efficiently is to perform a greater evil than not to educate our students at all. Many of the totalitarian regimes of the last century have been ruthlessly and expertly efficient in pursuing their plans of action. Their plans were, in that thin sense, good.

The Practical Question is more comprehensively practical than that. It asks not only about *how* to do what we happen to want to do. It also inquires whether what we want to do is *worth doing*, whether it is good and right and wise to do. It calls for scrutiny not only of the means to achieve predetermined political ends but also of the ends themselves. Therefore, it requires us to understand our society, our culture, our politics, and our ethics. Moreover, it prompts us to understand *ourselves* better, to inquire and discern what our true and best ends really are.

For example, if we take for granted that military force is justified whenever a foreign enemy threatens our national interests, then we will only ever inquire and learn about the means of national defense. But perhaps the assumption is not warranted. If we were to consult older, classical sources—thinkers such as Thomas Aquinas and Emer de Vattel—we would learn to think about national defense in terms of respect for human life, much as we think of personal self-defense. That might open our eyes to the more profound questions of morality and justice that are at stake in our national defense policies.

Or consider debates about a minimum wage. If we consider only the goal of increasing wages for working-class poor people, we might conclude that we are willing to sacrifice the lowest-paying jobs to achieve that goal. But we might consider a more nuanced policy when we consider the teenagers, college students, and other partly employed people whose jobs will be sacrificed, as well as thinking about the goods at stake. For example, we might observe that teenagers learn important virtues and life lessons by working a low-paying or part-time job. Indeed, some of the teenagers who could benefit the most morally from working in such jobs are those from middle-class and wealthy families who may never again have the opportunity to learn what life is like for the working poor.

PRACTICAL INQUIRY TOWARD PRACTICAL WISDOM

The thin version of the practical question is not unimportant. Indeed, it is implied in the thicker Practical Question. When we ask each moment, "What shall I do?", we generally inquire in light of larger projects, political goals, and life plans. The Practical Question concerns both means and ends. And it considers ends in the context of other, broader goals that we share with others, which are not found in our momentary feelings and desires, and which give meaning to our actions and our lives.

That we can ask the Practical Question and that we can learn from the practical inquiries of those who came before us suggests that we might be able to find the right answers. We just might reason together about what is right to do. And we might reason better if we consider how others have reasoned in the past.

To refuse to study the past is precisely *not* to be liberated from prejudices and bigotries. It is instead to succumb to our own, contemporary prejudices and bigotries and to remain enslaved in our doing to our appetites and instincts. To fail to consider the question is to act subrationally, in a way that is less than fully human. To ask the Practical Question along with Aristotle and Mother Teresa and others who came before is to make ourselves open to the possibility of being human.

To consider how others have answered the Practical Question is to make ourselves open to the possibility of becoming *fully* human. The educator Bradley Watson observes that for Plato, Aristotle, and Rousseau (and, we might observe, many other great thinkers), one goal of education is to make us less selfish and more truly ourselves. Through education, "the passions of the self are tamed and the individual made social."[8]

The Practical Question prompts us to look beyond our individual interests and fleeting feelings to search for practical wisdom. When we stop to consider the reasons for our actions, we perceive the value of understanding how successful plans have been pursued in the past *and* whether those plans promoted the common good of those people affected by them, overall and in the long run. Our pragmatic student, who wants only a technical education and a credential, does not yet know that she needs this kind of practical reason in order to be a fully flourishing human being. We need to show her how to answer both the thin and thick versions of the Practical Question. The Practical Question concerns our actions *now*—at this moment—because now is the only moment in which we can choose to deliberate and act. But to answer the Practical Question well requires our students to take the long view.

The Practical Question provides a way around the roadblock that our students have constructed on the road to understanding. As long as we stay in the realm of the purely theoretical, it is plausible to maintain that each of us has her own, personal truth and that none of us is in a position to judge another's truth. But that becomes implausible when we move to the realm of practical reason.

We can challenge our students to think practically about moral truth even in our classrooms, where we are engaged mostly in theoretical, abstract inquiries. We can motivate our students to consider important moral goods by examining moral controversies of the past and how people thought about them. The fact is that, when pressed by a practical imperative, students are unwilling to excuse grave wrongs. They all think it is wrong to captain a slave ship, for example. And they all believe that anyone who captains a slave ship should be held legally responsible.

When we inquire *why* they reach those judgments, students can provide real, honest-to-goodness *reasons*. They refer to considerations outside of their own preferences and desires. They refer to justice and to goods of health and moral agency, goods that slavery destroys. In this way, they reveal that they actually believe in objective standards of right judgment. They think that there are right answers to the Practical Question and that we can know them.

Getting to this self-revelation requires some work. At first, the reasons that students provide are not often good reasons. They are likely to argue that one should not engage in the slave trade because slavery is racist. Of course, this explanation is wholly inadequate to explain the judgment that slavery itself is wrong. One can easily expose the flimsiness of the racist trope by adding detail to the hypothetical, explaining that the slave owner and the slave are often members of the same race. Some other reason must explain the judgment that slavery is wrong.

Nevertheless, when students reveal to themselves their own inclination to reach for reasoned arguments when explaining their moral judgments, we have a solid starting place for fruitful inquiry. We can examine other possible reasons for not treating human beings as mere commodities, such as Immanuel Kant's imperative that one should always treat other people only as ends in themselves and never as mere means. We can examine the Jewish and Christian idea, given to us by Moses and Saint Paul, among others, that all human beings are equally created in the image of God; or the idea of natural law thinkers, articulated by philosophers such as Thomas Aquinas, John Finnis, and Mary Ann Glendon, that every human being has inherent dignity and worth. We can discuss John Stuart Mill's ideas about the value of liberty and Joseph Raz's ideas about the value of personal autonomy. *And* we can discuss the role of race and tribalism in conversation with Abraham Lincoln, Frederick Douglass, and Alveda King.

Suddenly, before they even realize it, our students are learning to reason from old women and dead men, maybe even Aristotle. And now the students begin to realize that those men and women are not especially bigoted; at least they are no more bigoted than our students. In fact, they are not even all that old or completely dead. Their insights live on in the moral judgments that my students are eager to render.

Here lies our hope. The Practical Question cannot always be avoided by reasoning agents, human beings. It is the aspect of human life that supplies our lives with meaning and purpose. We desire meaning and purpose. And we want to know what is right to do. So, let us ask the Practical Question, what is right to do. Let us ask it of our students and of ourselves. And let us think critically about it in conversation with those who have asked it well before.

NOTES

1. What follows in this section draws heavily from, and builds upon, the analytical philosophical tradition of jurisprudence revived at Oxford University and the University of Notre Dame in the middle of the twentieth century, especially H. L. A. Hart, *The Concept of Law* (3rd ed., Oxford University Press, 2012) (1st ed., 1961) and John Finnis, *Natural Law and Natural Rights, 3–22* (2nd ed., Oxford University Press, 2011) (1st ed., 1980).

2. See, for example, C. S. Lewis, *The Abolition of Man* (San Francisco: Harper Collins, 2001) (1944); Allan Bloom, *The Closing of the American Mind* (New York: Simon & Shuster, 1987); *Civic Education and Culture*, Bradley C. S. Watson, ed. (Wilmington, DE: ISI Books, 2005).

3. Lewis, 24–25.

4. Ibid., 27–33.

5. Ibid., 4.

6. Ibid., 30–40.

7. Josiah Bunting III, "Barbarians at the Gates: Enemies of Character," in *Civic Education and Culture*, Bradley C. S. Watson, ed. (Wilmington, DE: ISI Books, 2005), 157, 159–60.

8. Ibid., xv.

FIVE

Rights Without Duties, Wrongs Without Right

WRONGS AND RIGHTS

Our age is morally uncertain. We do not agree about what is right. We do not even agree where to look for right answers. Nevertheless, many people seem to be quite certain about one thing: They are certain that other people are wrong. Other people are wrong to believe that the law should restrict abortion or to believe that it should not restrict abortion; wrong to advocate for limits on carbon emissions or wrong not to support such limits; wrong to ingest marijuana or wrong to oppose the legalization of marijuana possession.

We see wrongs everywhere. Yet we cannot explain why we think other people are wrong if we cannot explain what is objectively right—right not only for us but also for them and for everyone else. We want judgment, but we have no standard by which to judge. We proliferate wrongs. However, we have no account of what is right to do. This is a dead end.

Even here, we can find a way to begin afresh. The very fact that we want to say that some acts are wrong entails that there is a right standard. We cannot reconcile all of these claims. Obviously, we are not all right. But we seem to think that there is such a thing as "wrong." And this implies that there is such a thing as "right." We agree on this much.

It turns out that we cannot do without concepts of right and wrong. The reason is that every one of us is confronted in each moment with the Practical Question: "What shall I do now?" And we need an answer to the Practical Question. We need to know what we must and should and may do—what is right to do—and we need to know what we must not

51

and should not and would be advised to not do—what is wrong to do. Rights and wrongs are indispensable.

This suggests a way forward for teachers, civic leaders, business executives, clergy, politicians, lawyers, and others who help shape our civic discourse. We can ask variations on the Practical Question as a way of motivating and productively directing an inquiry into moral questions. When we ask together "What is right to do?", we discover that we are offering (different) answers to the same question and supplying different provisions for the same human need. We do not all agree on what is to be done. That's what divides us. However, we all agree that it is important to know the answer. Moreover, increasingly, we think that there is a right answer to know. That's our common ground. We can start there.

In answering the Practical Question together, we reveal our inherent orientation toward knowledge of the right. Though we often disagree about what is right, the idea that there is such a thing as practical truth is a starting point for rebuilding our education and discourse. We might not agree on truth in the abstract. But at the bottom, nearly everyone can identify at least one act that they think is wrong to do, some idea that it is wrong to express, some way of life that is wrong to pursue. This shows that we believe there is such a thing as "right."

RIGHTS WITHOUT DUTIES

Indeed, we see rights everywhere. We assert the right to life, and the right to personal autonomy, and the right to be safe from hateful speech, and the right to free speech, and the rights of health care, public education, and student loans, and the right not to be taxed. As these few examples illustrate, we have an insatiable appetite for rights. But our "rights talk" (as Harvard law professor Mary Ann Glendon calls it) does not tell us who is responsible for our rights. As a result, all of our discourse about rights does not get us very far. The proliferation of rights without an account of what is wrong to do leads to the same dead end as the proliferation of wrongs without an account of what is right to do.

Imagine that you were to open the newspaper or click on your favorite news website one morning and were to read there a story about someone asserting a right to carrot cake. They love carrot cake so much they have initiated a lawsuit in federal court to vindicate their right. Explaining their decision to file the lawsuit against bakers, grocers, and government officials, the claimant has penned an editorial explaining why carrot cake is a fundamental human right that all people must respect.

Carrot cake is an important human good. It's a cake made of nutritious carrots. It's covered with cream cheese. And it's not dry and crumbly but rather full of moisture and compact, so it doesn't leave a mess all over the table. Now, you might happen to prefer other confections, the editorialist concedes. Perhaps you like pain au chocolat or sweet pies, those desserts of oppressive, Western colonial imperialism. Or perhaps you go in for angel food cake, a cake that is puffed up with superstitious religious presumption. But that's just your preference. You have no right to impose your views on others or to insist that carrot cake is any less legitimate than your preferred confection.

What's more, the editorial argues that carrot cake is central to the personal identity of many people. Some people love carrot cake so much that they serve it at their weddings. They celebrate birthdays, promotions, and other special occasions with carrot cake. They serve carrot cake to their house guests and bring it to office parties. Thus, carrot cake constitutes an essential aspect of their personal identity. Therefore, they must not be deprived of it. Any actions that substantially burden access to carrot cake infringe the basic right of human dignity. Any efforts to regulate carrot farmers, any subsidies for angel-food-cake bakers, and any failure by grocers to stock cream cheese are unconstitutional. Lovers of carrot cake must have a remedy for such wrongs.

For example, anyone who opens up a bakery, restaurant, coffee shop, or other commercial enterprises where baked goods are served is well advised to have lots of carrot cake on offer. To serve biscuits and scones but no carrot cake is discriminatory. Anyone who perpetrates such a grievous injustice against lovers of carrot cake deserves public disapprobation, civil liability, and reeducation in the virtues of orange vegetable confections. To offer to satisfy others' desires for banana bread and apple strudel without also satisfying the editorialist's desire for carrot cake on equal terms is to flout the inherent equality of all identarian interests and appetites.

Reading this editorial, you would no doubt check the date. Surely this is an April Fools' Day joke. Or perhaps you had mistakenly found your way to a satire. But if this is satire, it sounds familiar enough to be recognizable. You've heard something like it before. In fact, our legal and political discourse is full of assertions that are similar in form and substance to the assertion of a right to carrot cake, if less trivial. Contemporary rights discourse—even rights adjudication—elevates the peripheral and minor at the expense of the central and fundamental.

For example, a few years ago, the Constitutional Council of France ruled that access to the Internet is a fundamental human right of which a person cannot be deprived but can only be forfeited as punishment after due process and a conviction. The Council ruled that the fundamental right of Internet access rendered unconstitutional a democratically enacted law. That law authorized Internet service providers (ISPs) to terminate service to those who used the Internet to steal copyrighted works. The purpose of the law was, of course, to prevent people from taking what does not belong to them. But the Council ruled that copyright thieves cannot be punished by depriving them of the tools they are using to steal.

The Council reasoned that Internet access is a primary means by which people communicate in the twenty-first century and that it is, therefore, an instrumental support for the right of free expression. But this is fallacious. People who steal other people's intellectual property are not using the Internet for self-expression. They are stealing someone *else's* self-expression. And though their loss of Internet access deprives them of one means to communicate, they have others. The fundamental right at stake is not the right to have Internet access. It is the right to communicate.

The ability to communicate is not entirely contingent on Internet access. Someone who has lost their Internet access has not been thwarted in their expression as comprehensively as someone who has been imprisoned for criticizing their government. Nor is the legal or constitutional weight of these "rights" the same. A government that silences political dissenters perpetrates a grave injustice, both as a matter of legal justice and natural law. A service provider that protects intellectual property by shutting off access to thieves under authority of the law is performing an act of legal justice by means that are rationally related to the wrong it is charged to prevent.

Even if we think that Internet access is equally as important as free political expression, that does not make it a *right*. Indeed, what kind of a right could the right to have Internet access be? It's not a legal right. It is not mentioned in the French Constitution or the Universal Declaration of Rights. By contrast, a copyright *is* a legal right, secured both by the positive law of France and by international law. From a legal perspective, the decision is not only plainly wrong but plainly backward.

Nor is the right of Internet access a universal human right. What meaning could such a right have in South Sudan or North Korea, where people lack basic necessities such as food and personal security? One cannot have a right to a resource that does not exist. Just as it would have been nonsense to assert a right to telephone access in the eighteenth century, it is nonsense to speak of a right of Internet access across much of the world today.

Furthermore, the right of Internet access cannot be an absolute, or even categorical, right. Just as people use the Internet for good and just ends, many people use it for unjust and illegal ends. If courts deprive authors and artists and musicians of the legal means to sanction piracy, then the best of those creators, whose creations cost the most money to produce and distribute, have strong incentives to stop creating. In that case, intellectual property thieves may keep their access to the Internet but the Internet would no longer be worth accessing.

The right to access the Internet is contingent on the rights of those very people whose losses the law was intended to remedy. It is also conditional on other considerations, such as the degree of access, the means and technologies by which access is delivered, the content one has access to, and other preconditions of Internet use. These are necessarily contingent upon circumstances. Several different factors have the potential to deprive people of meaningful Internet access, and almost none of them infringe anyone's rights.

The resonance of the carrot-cake editorial and the French Council's decision show that our rights discourse is inflated. The ubiquity of rights talk is a leveler. When everyone asserts a right to everything, no one has a right to anything. Rights do not correlate with concrete duties, so no one bears responsibility for others' rights. I may have a right to carrot cake, but no one has a duty to make one for me. My right to Internet access doesn't mean anything without Internet service providers, content creators, computers, and inventors and producers of all the technology needed to make the Internet work.

When we assert rights contrary to the law, we threaten to destroy civil rights. "Rights" such as Internet access are often used to avoid responsibility to obey the law and ignore our legal duties, as the French Council decision demonstrates. For the flip side of one person's right is another person's duty. What one person is obligated to do because of his duty is what another person is owed because of his right. Because our legal duties are the corollaries and content of other people's legal rights, to void duties is to void rights.

To see how hazardous the inflation of rights has become, compare the right to access the Internet with the right not to be trafficked. Both rights are now said to be fundamental. Yet these rights are not similar. Unlike the right to Internet access, the right not to be trafficked is codified in the positive laws of nearly every country and is enshrined in constitutions around the world. It is both universal and absolute. It has the same meaning everywhere, and it cannot be justified for any reason. It is always wrong to sell a human being. Period. The right to have Internet access has none of those attributes.

Estimates vary widely, but at least several thousand people, and perhaps many more, are trafficked in France each year. The French government is able to identify about 1,000 victims annually.[1] However, there is almost certainly many times that number. Human trafficking sadly is ubiquitous worldwide. And traffickers and victims are often hard to identify.

To protect vulnerable people, many political communities have enacted laws specifying criminal sanctions for those who participate in the sex trade. These laws secure at least two fundamental rights: the right not to be trafficked and the right not to do wrong. Both of those rights are at stake when a young girl is coerced into prostitution. Sex trafficking violates both her personal autonomy and her moral integrity. Because both of those rights are so fundamental and important, many political communities have decided to express their disapprobation of prostitution, to make it more costly to pursue and, thus, decrease demand, and to incapacitate those who exploit vulnerable young people.

Until recently, Canada was among those nations. The people of Canada had enacted laws securing the common-law prohibition against prostitution, a prohibition that is centuries old and is part of the fundamental laws of both common-law (i.e., law inherited from England by her former colonies) and civil-law nations (i.e., Roman law passed by Continental nations, such as France and Spain, to their colonies). In short, the right not to engage in prostitution is ancient and universal. But in a 2013 decision, the Supreme Court of Canada ruled that laws prohibiting prostitution infringe the right of personal security. Freedom to engage in prostitution is not a constitutional right in Canada. But the Court identified it with the right of security of the person, a fundamental right that is secured by the Charter of Rights. On this ground, the Court invalidated laws prohibiting the sex trade.

Granted, one might form the prudential judgment that laws prohibiting prostitution are overprotective of trafficking victims. After all, some women might choose to engage in prostitution, and laws that make it more risky and costly for their clients to transact with them burden their liberty to act as they wish. But this not does entail that prostitution is a worthwhile option for them, much less that one has a right to hire or serve as a prostitute.

Furthermore, not all women who are engaged as prostitutes choose prostitution. Many young women who are hired out as prostitutes are being exploited by others. The law is designed to protect them. Why should the liberty interest of willing prostitutes be used to destroy legal protections for unwilling prostitutes, whose absolute rights are, in fact, being infringed? The assertion that one has a *right* to avoid the reach of antiprostitution laws has the foreseen effect of depriving vulnerable young people of the protection of antiprostitution laws—laws that secure fundamental rights not to be sexually exploited and not to be forced to do wrong. This makes a mockery of the very idea of rights.

Therefore, we have a problem. We are spending down the normative currency of rights in Western legal and political discourse. The term now used to describe trivial desires and instrumental means of self-expression and self-actualization is the same term that has long been used to describe rights not to be defamed, raped, or subjected to other harmful wrongdoing. Instrumental, peripheral, and even trivial preferences trade on the normative currency of basic, central, and fundamental rights. By inflating our rights discourse, we devalue fundamental rights.

One result of this rights inflation is that rights are no longer conclusive and authoritative. They are instead defeasible and contingent, like advice instead of orders. This renders rights less meaningful as guides to deliberation and judgment. Rights are now in conflict with each other. Two people claim rights, but ultimately, only one of them will be vindicated as the right. One sees this in the French Internet access case and the Canada prostitution case. The "right" of intellectual property thieves to express themselves on the Internet defeats the legal right of intellectual property creators to commercialize their creations. The "right" of some prostitutes to find clients more easily defeats the legal right of other young women not to be exploited.

And that is not the only problem. For though the normative value of rights is spent down, we still must engage in practical deliberations about what is to be done. If we can no longer resort to rights to tell us which preferences should prevail—because all preferences are now rights— then we will resort to other considerations.

When everything is a right, nothing is. And our moral, political, and legal discourse will now be guided by something other than rights. At best, we will make practical decisions based on considerations of the common good. But more usually, especially when we cannot agree, we will be controlled by the personal opinions and feelings of the loudest people at the expense of the common good and at the expense of the real, fundamental rights of the voiceless.

WRONGS WITHOUT RIGHT

To have rights without correlative duties is not to have rights at all. It is only to have demanding people who are easily aggrieved. We have become a demanding people. And we are aggrieved without end. As a result, we see wrongs everywhere.

We are surrounded by moral judgment everywhere, on all sides, all the time. Despite the moral chaos and confusion of our age, everyone seems to be quite certain that other people are going about their lives wrongly. Indeed, we now have cottage industries devoted to expressing outrage at all the wrongs we suffer.

Consider, for example, controversies about speech on college and university campuses, where we find groups of faculty and students devoted to the eradication of what they call "hate speech." This category of speech includes racist expressions, such as assertions of white supremacy. But it also includes criticisms of Islamist political ideology, arguments in favor of immigration laws, and any expression of the view that marriage is by nature the union of a man and woman. These views are not hateful (though some people might express them in hateful ways). Yet faculty and students on several campuses have demanded that all speakers espousing those views must be prohibited from appearing on campus. And some activist groups attempt to silence people who express those views publicly by labeling them "hate groups" and pressuring public and civic institutions to disassociate from them.

Sometimes they succeed. Ayaan Hirsi Ali is a Somali-born scholar and activist who was born and raised Muslim. She condemns the practice of female genital mutilation that occurs in some Muslim communities, a wrong that she suffered as a child, and she expresses concern that allowing mass immigration from certain Muslim countries facilitates human trafficking and other crimes against the vulnerable. A few years ago, Brandeis University rescinded a speaking invitation to Ali after faculty and students protested. Around the same time, the activist organization Southern Poverty Law Center (SPLC) added Ali to its "hate list," labeling her an "anti-Muslim extremist." Shortly thereafter, Ali was forced to cancel other speaking engagements.

None of Ali's critics showed her statements to be false or motivated by hatred. They simply labeled her ideas "hate" or "Islamophobic" and silenced her on that ground. As this example illustrates, the putative right not to be exposed to offensive speech is used to infringe on the real, fundamental rights of thoughtful and well-spoken people to express facts and opinions that are unpopular.

One striking feature of the expressions of outrage we now frequently witness is that the outraged victim seldom stops to ask whether he or she has done wrong, much less what would be a right response to the speech that offends them. Faculty and students who prevent the expression of unpopular ideas in public events send a strong signal to minority students that their dissenting views are not welcome in the classroom. By silencing certain opinions and marking certain questions out of bounds, they impoverish education for everyone.

Meanwhile, speakers who go out of their way to offend and who provoke their interlocutors intentionally coarsen our discourse. They impart to young people the lesson that the quickest way to attract attention and fame is to express one's views in the most outrageous manner possible and to hide behind their civil right to speak. They have more in common with the mob than with Ayaan Hirsi Ali.

RECOVERING THE RIGHT

It turns out that we cannot do without concepts of right and wrong. The reason is that every one of us is confronted in each moment with the Practical Question. And we need an answer to the Practical Question. We need to know what we must and should and may do—what is right to do—and we need to know what we must not and should not and would be advised to not do—what is wrong to do.

Throughout most of the history of Western law, until very recently, a right is not essentially an entitlement. Much less is it simply what one happens to want. A right is instead a direction for the action of real people who must decide how they are to act. To say that one has a right to free speech means that others have a duty to refrain from preventing one from communicating. To say that one has a right to life is to say that others have a duty not to kill. To say that one has a right to limbs is to say that others have a duty not to maim. And to say that one has a right not to be trafficked is to say that others have a duty not to enslave or sell for sex.

As these examples show, a right is an answer to the Practical Question, "What shall I do?" It is a reason, a conclusive reason. A right is what is right to do or refrain from doing regarding another person or class of persons or all persons. Its meaning is in identifying what duty I owe the person who is to be affected by my action or failure to act. It binds us. It imposes obligation.

Today, we tend to speak of "rights" as what belongs to us or what we are entitled to have or receive. But for most of human history, "rights" referred to what we owe other people. A right is either the right action to be taken or the possession of another person that is not to be infringed. In both kinds of cases, the point of a right is to identify our own duty toward someone else.

This tradition of thinking about the right goes back many centuries. In 1215, the bad English King John was required to sign Magna Carta, making assurances that he would not deprive people of their ancient customs, their property, and their liberty except according to the law of the land. The meaning of the rights of English common law, which the American founders later invoked in the Declaration of Independence, is—consists precisely in—the King's duties and obligations toward his countrymen.

Long before King John, the ancient Greek philosopher Plato revolutionized Western thought by writing books about his teacher, Socrates. Those accounts reveal that Socrates was always asking questions about what is right and just to do. (Indeed, asking questions is one of Socrates' greatest legacies. Today, we refer to the method of teaching by asking questions as the Socratic method.) To say that an action was right or just was to say that it is the right thing to do. To say that it is wrong or unjust is to say that it is not to be done. Socrates wanted to know which actions were which.

After his unjust conviction for corrupting the youth of Athens by asking too many questions, Socrates sat in captivity with his friend Crito. Crito visited Socrates on the last day before Socrates' execution to urge him to flee Athens. Crito assured Socrates that not only Crito but also other friends stood ready to enable the escape.

This suggestion troubled Socrates' mind. He asked Crito to help him think through the right answer to the Practical Question: "What should I do?" Socrates was not prepared to act until he had settled his mind on which course of action was just (i.e., right) and with which was unjust (i.e., wrong).

If it is right for Socrates to stay in Athens and face punishment, then he has a duty to stay. Crito reminds Socrates that he, too, has rights, and that the Athenians have acted unjustly toward him. If the Athenians have deprived Socrates of his right to an impartial trial, then they have infringed their duty to afford him such a trial. Socrates does not deny that he has been unjustly condemned. But that does not give him a right to flee Athens and avoid his punishment. He reminds Crito that he lived in Athens for many years before his trial, enjoying the benefits of the law. The laws of Athens made it possible for him to live an active, productive, and enjoyable life. Socrates teaches that it would be ungrateful and unjust for him to flout the laws of Athens now, having reaped all the benefits that the laws afforded for so many years.

As Socrates taught, the correct notion of a "right" is not self-focused; it is focused on our duties toward others. Another ancient text teaches this lesson from a religious perspective. In the Gospel of Jesus Christ according to Luke, Jesus is reported to have taught in parables. One of the most famous parables concerns a young man whom we now refer to as the Prodigal Son. This young man has a wealthy father. He approaches his father and demands what he thinks is rightfully his—the inheritance he expects to receive when his father dies. "Father, give me the share of property that is coming to me." The boy is asserting his rights to the fullest extent. His father complies, dividing his estate between his two sons. The young son then leaves. He travels to a "distant country," where he spends his entire inheritance on parties and "reckless living."

At this point in the story, the young son is thinking about his rights the way that most Westerners today think of rights—as entitlements and satisfactions. He wants the half of his father's estate that one day will belong to him. His concern is getting what he wants. He is indifferent as to who will bear the price of his satisfaction. Whether the money comes from his father or somewhere else is not important to him. Indeed, his father is not important to him. He values his father primarily for the money his father will be worth when he is dead.

Things do not go well for the young son. After spending all he had, the son finds himself in a land far from home, which is now suffering a famine. He finds a job feeding pigs. He is so hungry that he longs for some of the pig food. The parable continues thus:

> But when he came to himself, he said, "How many of my father's hired servants have more than enough bread, but I perish here with hunger! I will arise and go to my father, and I will say to him, 'Father, I have sinned against heaven and before you. I am no longer worthy to be called your son. Treat me as one of your hired servants.'" And he arose and came to his father.[2]

Now the young son is thinking about his rights in the correct sense. He is asking what is right for him to do. And he is suddenly aware of his father, not only as a potential source of cash and property but also as a person who is owed respect. He realizes that he has wronged his father—

he says he has sinned against him—and that his dire circumstance is his own fault. He hopes that his father will show him mercy and allow him to work on the family estate. But he dares not hope that his father will restore him to his status as son, with rights to share his father's wealth. He recognizes that he forfeited these rights by demanding the inheritance that would be his after his father's death.

The parable then takes a surprising turn. As the son is walking home, "his father saw him and felt compassion, and ran and embraced him and kissed him." The father then breaks out the best food and drink and throws a party to celebrate. "For this my son was dead, and is alive again; he was lost, and is found."

Disregarding his own rights, the father shows love and compassion to his son. The father forgives. His son has wronged him, preferring the father's wealth to his company and squandering even his wealth. Nevertheless, the father restores his son to a status that the young son casually relinquished in exchange for a licentious lifestyle and which he no longer deserves. Because the father wants what is good for his son, he does not insist on his own rights. And as a result, he and his son are reconciled.

The lesson of these ancient texts is that the right thing to do is not always to insist on the satisfaction of our own rights. We go wrong when we think of rights primarily as our entitlements. Instead, we should think of rights as guides for practical reasoning. Rights are useful to help us to live together in the community, to do natural and legal justice to each other. But they work well only when they answer the Practical Question. Their job is not to make sure we get what we prefer or want. Their job is to direct us on what to do.

FUNDAMENTAL RIGHTS

To make rights work well, we need to recover meaningful rights, rights that can do the job of helping us live together well. We can begin to recover meaningful rights by examining assertions of right from the perspective of *duty*. This is another way to say that we should examine rights using the Practical Question: "What shall I do?" Properly functioning rights are not primarily about what I am owed or to what I am entitled. Rather, they direct my own action. If everyone were attentive to his or her duties, then they would be attentive to other people's rights. And then everyone's rights would be respected.

By examining rights from the point of view of the duties with which they correlate, we can tell the difference between central or strong instances of rights and peripheral or weak instances. We can separate real rights from imposters that trade on the normative prestige of real rights and which devalue liberty and equality for all. And we can distinguish different senses of "rights," especially the difference between rights that are fundamental and universal and those that are contingent and fact-dependent.

In contemporary discourse, we refer to the most central, universal, and important rights as "fundamental rights." One has no fundamental right to eat carrot cake. And there is no fundamental right to engage in prostitution or have Internet access. However, the weakness and contingency of those claims does not mean that there are no fundamental rights. In fact, we can know what fundamental rights people have because we can know what fundamental duties we owe each other. Certain duties are so important and universal that they give rise to rights that all societies must respect and secure. For example, we all have duties not to enslave all other people. Therefore, everyone has a fundamental right not to be enslaved.

The first thing to observe is that a right must impose some particular disadvantage on some particular person. Each right comes with a price, and someone must pay it. If it is to be a meaningful guide to practical deliberation and choice, and not merely a rhetorical device, a right must impose on some identifiable person a duty, liability, or other burden. It is the disadvantage—the duty or other burden—borne by the other person, that gives the right its meaning and content.

Consider a simple example, a right that is not fundamental but only involves two people. Suppose you operate a sandwich shop. I enter your shop and place down cash equivalent to the cost of a ham sandwich. I now have a legal right to receive the sandwich from you. What that means is that you have a duty to make a ham sandwich for me.

This is a simple and particular right. It is context-specific and conditional. You have no obligation to take my money or make a ham sandwich for me if you have just run out of ham. Nor do you have a duty to provide a ham sandwich to anyone if you are kosher. Your right not to violate your conscience defeats my uninformed expectation that I might acquire a ham sandwich. Just as I have no fundamental right to have my carrot cake and eat it too, there is no universal or fundamental right to a ham sandwich. Your duty is the sense and meaning of my right to a ham sandwich. Without your duty, my "right" has no sense or meaning.

By comparison, fundamental rights are more general and universal. We can see such rights also by considering our duties. Think about our duty to exclude ourselves from things that we do not own. Each of us bears this duty. When walking through a parking lot to your car, you pass many other automobiles.[3] Some of them are nicer and more expensive than yours. And you might be able to put some of those cars to better use than their owners will. In fact, some owners of some of those cars might be planning to use their cars to commit wrongs—to carry on an extramarital affair, or to serve as getaway driver for a crime. None of that matters to you as you consider your duties concerning the cars. The cars are not yours. Therefore, you have a duty not to enter or take them.

Because you have that duty, all of the owners of the cars have the right to exclude you. To say that you have a duty to exclude yourself from things other people own *just is* to say that they have a right to exclude you. In other words, it is to acknowledge one of the basic rights of private property. Notice that this right is universal and ineradicable. Even in communist societies and other collectivist tyrannies, people have duties to exclude themselves from things they do not own. Communist countries do not (and cannot) eradicate private property duties. They merely arrogate all of the correlative private property rights to the governing elites who control the Communist Party and government. (This is why, despite the rhetoric of their leaders, Communist societies are actually *less* equal than societies that have private property and other civil liberties.)

We can perceive other fundamental rights in the same way, by examining them from the perspective of their correlative duties. While writing this book, I have a conclusive reason—a duty—not to libel people. If I were to make false statements about Ayaan Hirsi Ali, for example, and those statements were to cast her in a bad light or disparage her in some way, then I would be performing a wrong, the opposite of a right. That is to say, Ayaan Hirsi Ali has a right not to be defamed by me.

This right is fundamental and universal. Notice that Ali has the same right not to be defamed by anyone else, and I have the same right not to be defamed by her. And our mutual rights are not contingent. It would be wrong for me to defame Ali whether or not I promised not to libel and slander her, just because we are both human beings. The right not to have one's reputation falsely stolen is as fundamental and universal as the right not to have one's private property stolen. It is fundamental in the way that the right to have Internet access cannot be. The right not to be trafficked is fundamental in the same way.

As these examples show, a fundamental right correlates with a duty of abstention. A duty of abstention binds us not to act in a certain way. A duty to abstain from acting—to abstain from defaming or enslaving or stealing—can be universalized on the same terms for everyone. It need not be contingent on circumstances or conditional upon consent or agreement. One has the same duty to everyone not to lie about them, exploit them, or take their things, and one can satisfy that duty the same way in all circumstances toward all people: by doing nothing. And similarly, the correlative right can be the same for everyone insofar as everyone operates under the same duty. Because everyone has the same duties *not* to enslave everyone else and *not* to take their things, everyone has fundamental rights of liberty and property.

Fundamental rights are rights to be left alone. Therefore, fundamental rights are sometimes called "negative rights." However, that term is a bit misleading. For as the case of prostitution shows, fundamental rights require legal security, and that requires affirmative powers to obtain redress. It is better to refer to them by their jurisprudential terms—liberties and immunities. One is at liberty when no one has the right to interfere with one's actions. One has an immunity when no one has the power to impose on one a liability for acting. Liberties and immunities are rights not to suffer intentional harm or unlawful burdens, and they impose on all of us fundamental duties not to harm or burden others.

By contrast to fundamental rights are claims and entitlements. These include claims to have carrot cake and Internet access as well as entitlements to receive an education. These are rights to be provided some good or satisfaction. They are not universal. They must be created by some law, either a private law such as a conveyance or contract or a public law such as a statute. They are inherently contingent and conditional, for they always require someone's action. One can honor another person's right to life by doing nothing to them. But one cannot honor another person's right to receive an education without doing something.

Also, claims and entitlements must have specified limits because they require an expenditure of resources. How much and what kind of education you are entitled to receive depends on what your abilities are, whether anyone is available to teach you, what the needs of society are at present, how much money the rest of us have available to pay for your education, and much else. For the same reasons, the right to have Internet access or health insurance or ham sandwiches or . . . is meaningless in a country with no resources.

To assert claims and entitlements as fundamental, such as a "right" to carrot cake or Internet access, is to render central and universal rights less meaningful. By contrast, real fundamental rights not to be wrongly harmed are indispensable guides to action. In answer to the Practical Question, it is always correct to answer, "Don't wrong that person!" Do not take the bread out of her mouth or force her to sell herself. Do not maim him, enslave him, or kill him. Those actions are never to be done.

FREEING OUR MINDS BY REASONING PRACTICALLY

Absolute wrongs such as those are few. Most of the time, the Practical Question is directed not at avoiding some inherent wrong but rather at determining some worthwhile action. Here things get more complicated. This is because our time and resources are limited. And there are so many good options to pursue. We cannot do all good things. We can only do some. Therefore, we must choose.

To choose well, we need to judge well. And we need to act effectively. However, before we can judge and act, we need to know. We need to know what our options are. We need to know which options are good and which are evil, what resources we have at our disposal, what abilities we possess, and what is the most efficient way to achieve our goals. We need to know who is in need and what their needs are. We must move beyond right and wrong to know the good and the effective.

The Practical Question presupposes the idea of knowledge. We can ask, for example, "What shall I do in this class room [or laboratory, or recital hall, or greenhouse, or playing field, etc.] now, during our time together?" This question is intelligible only if our act of asking it can lead us to some desirable goal, some valuable end for our mental efforts, some common objective for us to pursue together. And that is possible only if we can know it.

This is not necessarily to say that knowledge is something immutable and objectively true. It might be that the knowledge we pursue is merely contingent and instrumental. Perhaps we come together in the classroom to conduct some sort of transaction, in which we all give up some amount of personal autonomy to gain useful skills or abilities. We submit to the authority of the teacher and perform the tasks instructed on the syllabus, even when we do not feel like doing what the teacher instructs, only because we expect to get something tangible out of it, such as a better career or more earning power. Perhaps when we convene, we suspend our own personal preferences and projects temporarily so that we can be better equipped to pursue them after we leave. Perhaps we are just using each other, or tolerating each other, or achieving a Pareto-optimal exchange, as economists say.

Yet this might not be all that we are doing. Perhaps when we come together to learn we really are pursuing a common good, an end that we all share and that is both valuable for all of us and intelligible to all of us, individually and together: a good in its own right. Perhaps when we ask the Practical Question about our theoretical and scientific and artistic pursuits we all are participating together in something that is beneficial to all of us just for its own sake.

Whatever our motivations or reasons for pursuing this thing called knowledge—whether intrinsic or instrumental, contingent or enduring, common or personal—the idea of knowledge makes sense of what we are doing together. It answers the Practical Question.

- What shall we do in this law-school classroom? We shall pursue knowledge of the law through critical engagement with judicial opinions.
- What shall we do in this recital hall? We shall pursue knowledge of beauty through excellent performance of music.
- What shall we do in this laboratory? We shall pursue knowledge of chemistry through skillful experimentation.
- What shall we do as we plan this business venture? We shall pursue knowledge of how to deliver quality goods and services to our customers.

- What shall we do in this incident response training? We shall pursue knowledge of how to save lives and alleviate suffering in the event of a natural disaster.

Notice that some of these are theoretical pursuits with no immediate, practical payoff. Law students do not read old cases to advise a client about a particular case. They read old cases to understand the concepts and doctrines of law. Students study general rules and all-things-considered rules of thumb to acquire general knowledge of their fields, some of which they might never use in practice.

Nevertheless, even the theoretical pursuits of the classroom, practice room, and laboratory have practical points. The student studies to acquire knowledge, forms of understanding that are valuable to have, either in their own right or because they are instrumentally valuable for other purposes, or both. The student who expresses (healthy, open-minded) skepticism of Einstein's theory is doing something important *both* because she comes better to understand the theory *and* because she might discover a flaw or limitation of the theory that will have practical consequences if we prepare to send spaceships beyond Mars to other parts of the universe.

How we learn and deliberate has consequences. While careless study might not always have the same immediate consequences as careless practical inquiries, eventually we will suffer bad consequences in our practical deliberations and actions if we do not learn well. Bad math causes bridges to collapse and rockets to explode. Bad medical schools produce bad doctors, who commit malpractice.

Therefore, the Practical Question matters in our theoretical inquiries, and our theoretical inquiries matter in our practical pursuits. This is because the pursuit of knowledge is a practical pursuit in itself and because theoretical knowledge often has practical implications. We have reasons to get our answers right, to be correct. In other words, we have practical reasons to pursue truth. However, truth is a contested idea in our time. In the next chapter, we consider where to look for it.

NOTES

1. https://www.state.gov/j/tip/rls/tiprpt/countries/2018/282656.htm.
2. Luke 15:17–20 (English Standard Version).
3. This illustration comes from J. E. Penner, *The Idea of Property in Law*, 74–77 (Oxford: Oxford University Press, 1997). I have built on Penner's insights (and the insights of others) to build a moral case for property rights and duties in Adam J. MacLeod, *Property and Practical Reason* (Cambridge: Cambridge University Press, 2015).

SIX

The Idea of Truth

There must be an answer to the Practical Question, a practical truth about which we are to inquire. For we cannot think that there is no truth without working our way into hopeless confusion. One cannot rationally maintain the claim that there is no practical truth to be pursued in answer to the practical question of whether to pursue truth.

If one says, "There is no truth," then one is making a truth claim—a claim about what is true. One is positing a proposition for acceptance on the ground that the proposition conforms to reality. The claim that there is no truth is a theoretical statement. But it is also a practical statement in response to the Practical Question, "Should I believe in truth?" Implied in the statement is that you would be mistaken to deny that there is no truth. By the very act of stating, "There is no truth," one has demonstrated that there *is* truth, truth about the nonexistence of truth.[1]

Further evidence of the existence of truth is found in the fact that people criticize others' beliefs as false. Person A says, "I believe x." Person B says, "You might believe x, but I do not believe x." The proposition x is independent of either person's belief in it. Person B is claiming that proposition x is not worthy of her belief in it, even though Person A believes it. Implicit in this criticism is that belief is not enough to have genuine knowledge. To count as knowledge, a belief must conform to reality. In other words, it must be true.

Truth is the difference between belief and knowledge. A belief is something one forms for oneself. Knowledge is a belief that corresponds correctly to its object. I may believe in leprechauns. However, I can only have knowledge about some person who exists. My belief in the existence of leprechauns is false unless leprechauns exist. By contrast, my belief in the existence of my wife is true because she exists in reality.

Like beliefs, opinions can be true or false. They can also be more or less true. One might form the opinion that Michael Jordan is the greatest basketball player in human history. Another person might rationally criticize that opinion as more or less valid in light of the available facts. Different people might look at the same evidence—championships won, total assists and points scored, performance of teammates—and form different judgments. However, no one would take seriously the idea that Mr. Bean, the inept, comic character of the eponymous movies, is the best basketball player ever. That opinion would be plainly false, which is to say untrue. Mr. Bean does not exist, except as whimsical fiction. That fact alone is incompatible with his being the best basketball player in history.

By criticizing beliefs and opinions as false, people prove that they understand truth of some kind to be real. Whatever one calls it, *truth is the standard by which beliefs and opinions are properly evaluated.* Some people might think that only mathematical and scientifically verifiable facts can be true. Others might think that moral propositions can be true, such as, for example, that lying is wrong because it deprives people of true knowledge. We might still disagree about the character and extent of truth. However, the very act of disagreeing about this question shows that we all think there is a truth to be known about truth.

Therefore, we should not waste much time or space on the idea that truth does not exist. The Practical Question presupposes the existence of an answer. It is our job to find it. Fine. But where are we to find truth?

We must face the fact that people disagree about a great many things that they think are true. And they appeal to a great variety of authorities. The fact of moral disagreement is itself true, and any attempt to locate truth must account for it. Even accepting that the Practical Question must have an answer, we can get bogged down trying to decide where to look for it if our sources of truth do not account for our differences.

People around the world and throughout history have proffered many different, possible places to find truth. To consider all these possibilities might be disorienting. However, if we examine them from a higher level of abstraction, we might discern patterns. We can group the potential locations of truth into a few categories, or ideas about truth. We might then examine those ideas about truth that most frequently arise.

Five ideas about truth arise with enough frequency that we can benefit from focusing on them.

1. **Truth is subjective experience.** Some hold the view that all truth is relative to the subjective experiences of different people. On this view, the feelings of each person are, for each person, what can be ultimately known.

2. **Truth is determined thought.** Another idea is that thought and belief are determined by material substance. Belief that there is truth to be found, like any other thought, is on this view the product of a material cause. Perhaps it is a curiosity gene. Or perhaps it is what we ate for breakfast or some other environmental cause.
3. **Truth is conventional.** A third idea is that truth is determined by convention. This idea is that truth is what "we" (however "we" is defined) decide it is. To search for truth is on this view to examine our customs, traditions, agreements, practices, artifacts, and institutions for evidence of what we do and what we believe.
4. **Truth is chosen.** A fourth idea is that truth is determined by personal choice and self-realization. On this view, truth is found in individual acts of choice that constitute reality.
5. **Truth is objective.** A final idea is that truth is determined by nature and found by reason. To take this idea seriously would lead us to try to understand human nature and the reasons for which human beings act.

Having narrowed the possibilities to these five, we still must evaluate them. Because space and time are short, and because you are still reading this book (and, therefore, are at least open to the idea that we can reason together about what is right to do), let us stipulate that we should *reason* our way through this evaluation. We should not flip a coin, or choose the option that makes us feel good, or take a vote. We should choose the option that is most justifiable on the grounds of available evidence and reasoned argument.

If we adhere to that stipulation, we find that we have a common starting place. We can begin where rational inquiry has begun for thousands of years: noncontradiction. Reason's point of departure—its first principle—is that one cannot both maintain and deny the same proposition at the same time. And this is true. Try to refute it.

When we turn the principle of noncontradiction on our five options, we see that we can eliminate two of them right away. The first and second ideas are as problematic as the initial objection that there is no truth. The claim that all truth is subjective would itself need to be subjective to be consistent. But, if the claim is merely a subjective opinion based on personal experience and feeling, then no one who does not share the opinion or the feeling in which it is grounded has reason to accept it.

The claim that all beliefs are determined by material forces, such as genes and environment, also refutes itself when asserted. If all beliefs are determined, then it is not possible to choose to believe or disbelieve anything. But to assert that all beliefs are determined by material causes is to assert that other people *should choose to believe* that all beliefs are determined by material causes. Otherwise, why bother to assert it? To tell a person that their belief in truth is merely a natural function of causes they do not choose or control, such as their genes or their environment, is to assert that they should choose to believe that their beliefs are merely a natural function of causes they do not choose or control. That is incoherent.

Having eliminated two of our five possible sources of truth, we now turn to consider the other three in some detail.

TRUTH IS CONVENTIONAL

Some people think that practical truth is conventional, that it is right to do what we all agree on, the norms that we live by together in community. Every group of people, every association and religious community and commercial business, and every society has norms and conventions to which its members adhere. For members of the group or community or society, the conventions determine what is right (and wrong) to do.

Those of us who live in democracies are accustomed to this idea. We have experience with legislatures, unions, faculty senates, student government associations, and other institutions of democratic deliberation. We choose people to represent us in those institutions and empower them to enact rules that we all will live by. We accept that, as long as our representatives are chosen lawfully, are not corrupt, and as long as they honor their promise not to violate our constitutions and charters and other fundamental commitments as a community, what they decide will be right for us to do. If the legislature decides to make the speed limit on highways 65 miles per hour rather than 70 miles per hour, then it is right for us to drive no more than 65 miles per hour and wrong to drive 70.

Not all conventions are deliberated about and voted upon, even in a democracy. Some norms and conventions are established by custom and practice. For example, in a traditional classroom, it is customary to remain silent while the teacher or professor is speaking, and to indicate one's desire to speak by raising one's hand in the air. This is not a rule enacted by democratic means such as a majority vote. It is just the way we do things. We have always done it this way for as long as we can remember, and it works for us. This custom enables us to share knowledge and to learn effectively.

This is not to suggest that customs are undemocratic. On the contrary, a custom that survives for a very long time is itself evidence that people follow the custom reasonably and assent to it voluntarily. It seems reasonable to us that, if we want to learn anything, we should not all talk at once. It seems equally reasonable that the person who possesses the most knowledge in the room should have the authority to determine who speaks and when. We did not have to agree to those propositions expressly. We assent it to them tacitly. But that our assent is tacit rather than express does not make our assent any less free, reasonable, or voluntary. We are at liberty to do otherwise. But we don't because this way works well enough.

Customary rules such as these are conventional and contingent upon our continued assent. We could stop obeying the custom and invent a new way of doing things. We know this is possible because other communities have different customs. Some schools do not follow traditional classroom conventions. For example, in Montessori schools, students direct their own learning individually. Teachers do not lecture the students or question them as Socrates questioned his students but instead guide and facilitate their inquiries and exploration in whatever directions the students choose to go.

Therefore, education can be achieved by different means and by following different customs and conventions. Different communities adhere to different customs either because they have different goals or because different means of achieving the same goal (acquiring and passing on knowledge) seem best to them. Because customs and other conventions are contingent upon the voluntary assent of the members, the community can change its conventional norms when it decides that a different rule or a set of rules would help the community more effectively to achieve its goals.

We might make new rules by express agreement. We might get together and discuss alternative ways of teaching and learning. And we might decide that, to pursue education by more effective means, we need to change the rules governing how we learn. We can choose our conventions.

Even if we cannot all agree on what rules need to be changed and what the new rules should be, we can at least agree on the means and institutions and rules for changing the rules. We might agree to change the rules by majority vote, or by electing people to deliberate and vote on our behalf, or by choosing the smartest or wisest among us to decide what the rules shall be. Whether we decide to deliberate and make rules as a whole people, or to abide by the rules made by our elected representatives acting in a legislative body, or to simply obey the person whom we respect the most, we can make our conventional rules for ourselves as a group, community, or society.

The important thing to notice about conventional moral truth is that it is generally right for us. Whether a rule is established by customs or express agreements or legislative enactment or some other means, it is right for us to follow the rules and wrong for any of us to disobey the rules. What the convention tells us is right to do (such as that we should keep to the right lane on the road except to pass a slower driver, or that we should drive no faster than five miles per hour over the speed limit), that is what one should do. We owe to each other an obligation to adhere to our customs and conventions so that we can together pursue the common good. If everyone did their own thing and decided for themselves what was right, we could never cooperate together to achieve good ends.

For example, the good of knowledge makes it reasonable for us to come together to learn from those who possess knowledge. This requires obedience to the conventions of the classroom. Though the conventions might differ from classroom to classroom or school to school, the conventions bind those who attend the class.

A student in a traditional classroom, where the convention is to remain silent while the teacher is talking, should remain silent while the teacher is talking. A student in that setting who remains quiet and receives instruction from the teacher is a good student, and a student who interrupts the teacher and other students and does not listen is a bad student.

Meanwhile, in a different classroom setting, different conventions determine what actions are right and wrong and which students are behaving well and poorly. For example, an informal seminar is predicated on the conventions that the discussion shall flow freely and that propositions stated by the teacher should be questioned and challenged rather than silently accepted. In that setting, governed by the particular conventions of a seminar classroom, a good student is one who talks back to the teacher, not in a way that disrespects the teacher but rather showing respect for the teacher precisely by challenging the claims and propositions that the teacher has put on the table for consideration by the students.

When we say that the conventions of a group or community determine which actions are right and wrong and which students are good and bad, we do not mean that someone who disobeys the conventional rules is evil or inherently unjust. We simply mean that the person who flouts the conventional rules has put himself to some extent in opposition to the practices of the group or community and, therefore, is now acting contrary to the good that the group is trying to achieve. He is bad relative to the convention, just as someone who drives on the left in the United States is a bad driver.

This sense of right is contingent upon the custom or convention. A good seminar student might make a lousy student in a more traditional classroom setting because he is prone always to challenge the teacher's statements rather than passively accept them. Concerning conventional moral truth, what is right and wrong or good and bad in one setting governed by one set of conventional norms is simply different than what is rightly ordered in a different setting that is governed by different conventions.

This idea—that moral truth is determined by our agreement or conventions—goes a long way toward explaining our views about what is right and wrong to do. Nevertheless, it runs up against two limitations. First, not everyone in a community assents to the community's conventions, yet everyone is expected to obey them. One answer to this conundrum, which goes all the way back to Plato, is that people consent to the rules of a society, including the rules they do not like or agree with, by living within the society and enjoying the benefits of its order and culture. But not everyone consents. For not everyone is free to choose where to live.

A second limitation to the idea that moral truth is determined by a group's or society's conventions is that not all conventions are morally valid. We do not think that all conventional norms are simply and entirely true and right just because the group, community, or society has adopted them. Even if everyone in a particular society agreed that it is right to make war on neighboring societies, kill their people, and steal their things, it would not be right for members of that society to do those actions.

Some societies say that it is not wrong for human beings to own other human beings as slaves. Indeed, many, if not most, human societies throughout history have said that. Some have even concluded that it is right for some people to be slaves because that is what they are good for.

That a society adheres to the conventional practice of slavery does not make it right. Most of us in the West today do not think that slavery is right. Indeed, we think that slavery is inherently wrong whether or not any particular society adopts rules allowing it. If that is true, then conventions cannot be the ultimate measure of right and wrong.

Some might reply that the view that slavery is objectively wrong is itself merely a convention. But in that case, we would have no reason to insist that people should never practice slavery under any circumstances and in any place. The argument that slavery is always and everywhere unjust is valid not because most people happen to agree with it. (In fact, we do not know whether most people in the world do agree with it.) Arguments against slavery take as criteria of their own validity truths that are objective, universal, and not contingent upon convention or agreement.

In short, conventions do not by themselves determine right and wrong because conventions can be wrong. Conventional rules play an important part in directing us to right answers about what we should do and not do as members of, or guests within, particular communities. In this sense, customs and legislative rules can teach us what is right. We need rules to help us live together in peace and order. And we should learn from those rules how to get along with each other. However, we should not make the mistake of looking only at customary rules. For they might teach us falsehoods.

Chapter 6

TRUTH IS CHOSEN

Another way to search for moral truth is to look at what individual people choose. From this perspective, it does not matter as much whether we agree about what is right and wrong. Nor is it necessarily important that we get correct answers in some objective or universal sense. What matters is that people get to choose. In this view, the most basic truths about morality are (1) that people choose the answers from among a variety of possibilities, and (2) that the choice is not coerced by threats or oppression. When both of those conditions pertain, people have personal autonomy. And personal autonomy is, on this view, what really matters.

The power to exercise personal autonomy is an awesome power. It is the power to generate one's own moral obligations. A college student can choose to attend graduate school in English literature and, thus, generate new obligations to attend class, study, and pay her tuition. A busy professional can choose to promise to attend his friend's musical theater performance and, thus, create for himself a new obligation that he would not have owed to his friend but for the promise. As we go through our lives, we make our own moral reasons, generate duties to govern our future actions, and, in this way, author our own lives.

The important insight at work here is that human beings are moral agents. Moral agency can be exercised only by someone who has free will, unencumbered by external constraints. A person who lives in fear of threats or who anticipates that she will suffer bad consequences for disobeying another's will is not exercising her own moral agency; she is submitting to other forces upon her actions. To choose what is right and good for its own sake—because it is right and good—is precisely *not* to choose the right and the good out of fear of some painful or harmful consequence.

Indeed, some good ends can *only* be chosen freely, without coercion. Suppose Gus introduces himself to Fred at a party. Gus would like Fred to be his friend. So, he pulls out a gun, holds it to Fred's head, and instructs Fred, "Be my friend." Gus has just destroyed the possibility of achieving the good of friendship with Fred. Fear of losing his life has supplanted in Fred's deliberations the otherwise-possible option of forming a friendship with Gus. Fred might, at that moment, pretend to be friendly toward Gus, but his motivation will not be friendship.

Free choice is risky. But it has more potential to achieve what is good than coercion does. Had Gus left Fred free to choose friendship with Gus, it is not certain that they would have become friends. But having threatened Fred, Gus made it certain that Fred will fear and distrust him.

Coercion is sometimes justified to prevent or deter people from causing harm, or to punish those who commit harmful wrongs. In such cases, it is necessary, though perhaps undesired. When coercion is justified, it is justified not because it is good in itself but because it is necessary to preserve some good, such as the rule of law or human life. This is why coercion should be used sparingly (at least among adults) and should always be proportionate to the wrong being prevented or punished.

In addition to freedom *from coercion*, people should also have freedom *for valuable choices*. The moral philosopher Joseph Raz argues (influentially and persuasively among academic philosophers) that to exercise free choice, one must have both freedom from coercion and valuable options from which to choose.[2] If there is only one sensible thing to do, then as soon as one perceives its possibility and rationality, one does it. That is not a meaningful choice.

Consider our man Fred again. When Gus holds a gun to Fred's head, Fred has only one option. He must do what is necessary to preserve his life. He must extract himself from the situation without being shot. His agency is reduced to the instrumental rationality of forming and executing a strategy of survival. People who believe in the basic value of personal autonomy would say that Gus is acting wrongly not only (or even necessarily) by threatening to perform an inherently wrong act but because he has deprived Fred of meaningful and free choice.

The importance of free choice explains (at least part of) what is wrong about societies that allow slavery. If free choice is morally valuable, then slavery is wrong (at least in part) because it deprives slaves of their free will and of their opportunities to choose what they will do and not do. The slave does not obey his own will but the will of the master. And the master ensures that the slave has no options but the one action that the master wants the slave to perform.

This explanation for the wrongfulness of slavery gets to the heart of the matter. But is it the entire matter? We have reason to believe that free choice is not the whole truth about what is right to do, even in the case of slavery.

Consider someone who sells himself into slavery. Suppose that he never regrets his decision because he is the sort of person who does not want to make decisions for himself. He finds it stressful or cumbersome to make choices, and he prefers that other people make his choices for him. Therefore, he sells himself as a slave to someone who seems always to know the right thing to do. He trusts his new master's judgment more than his own, and he obtains money in the transaction. Suppose further that he does something virtuous with the money, such as pay for a poor child's education.

Is this transaction wrong? Yes, it is wrong, even though the new slave chose to become a slave and chose his new master. Both the master and the slave have acted wrongly because they have chosen to act contrary to the inherent dignity of the slave as a rational moral agent, a human being whose nature it is to reason and choose before acting. Both of them have acted contrary to what is right, and both suffer moral harm as a result.

The life of a voluntary slave is objectively worse off as a result of his choice to become a slave. His condition of slavery is inherently and fully incompatible with his nature as a human being. He has suffered a profound moral impoverishment. And he suffers this harm even though he chose to enter into his morally impoverished condition. That he chose servitude does not make his servitude any less wrong.

The moral condition of the master is also worse off. The act of asserting total dominion over the will of another human being corrupts the character of the master. To become accustomed to domination is to fall into some of the worst vices, especially pride and avarice. The Oxford scholar C. S. Lewis once remarked, "I reject slavery because I see no men fit to be masters."

Now, the advocate of personal autonomy might reply that what makes the transaction of voluntary slavery wrong is that the voluntary slave has eliminated his future choices. The one choice that is wrong is the choice to give up future choices. But that is arbitrary. Nearly all choices entail the loss of future options. Because our time and resources are limited, the choice of one option almost always forecloses other options. To choose just is to limit one's future choices by giving up all the options not chosen and all the options that would have been available as a result of those options.

Many of the most admirable choices consist of eliminating future options. We admire someone who remains faithfully committed to one person, or one career, or one cause for an entire lifetime. And we admire them in large part because that commitment costs them considerably. It requires them to forego other opportunities that they might have pursued along the way.

For example, for a man to choose to marry a woman is, at least in societies that do not allow polygamy, to choose not to marry all other women. To remain faithfully married to one person for an entire lifetime partly consists of "forsaking all others," in the words of the classic wedding vow. Yet we rightly celebrate weddings and marital faithfulness. Generally, to choose to become an architect is to choose not to become a doctor. Yet we celebrate successful architects. For all but the most extraordinarily talented people, to succeed as a professional athlete requires such effort and commitment that it is not also possible to succeed as a professional musician. And to choose to support the Boston Red Sox is to choose not to root for the New York Yankees (and vice versa).

To make a choice to foreclose future options is to make a momentous choice. And momentous choices can be either very good or very bad. The more future options one forecloses, the more morally significant is the present choice, the more admirable is a good choice, and the more tragic is a bad choice. Someone like William Wilberforce, who made political sacrifices in order to pursue the life goal of ending legal slavery in the British colonies, is a heroic figure precisely because of the options he eliminated from his future choosing. By contrast, someone who spends several years in professional school studying for a profession for which they are ill-suited is wasting not only time and money but also other opportunities. And that is a significant loss.

Furthermore, to freely choose to do something is not by itself to make the choice good or valuable. Indeed, as both Raz and the moral philosopher Robert George have pointed out, sometimes the fact that one freely chose to do an action makes the choice worse, more evil, or wrong.[3] For example, our laws reflect the insight that someone who commits deliberate murder is more culpable than someone who commits involuntary manslaughter. To freely and intentionally choose to kill another human being is a worse wrong than to choose to do something dangerous that happens to result in another person's death. Free choice does not make the action more admirable. It makes it worthy of greater disapprobation.

To make a choice is also to limit one's own freedom in another way. To choose most options is to choose to submit to the authority of the community of people who constitute the option. To choose is generally to relinquish some aspect of personal autonomy and to come under the governance of norms and practices developed and invented by others.

For example, to choose to become an athlete is to submit to the rules of the sport and the physical and mental disciplines that are necessary for excellent performance on the field of play, all as developed and designed by people other than oneself. Those conventions were formed in many cases over decades or even centuries. They were developed not by one person but by large numbers of people spanning several generations.

In order to have valuable options from which to choose, one must live in a society that provides those options. Individuals cannot by themselves produce valuable options for choice. Consider the choice between studying to become an architect and studying to become a soldier. Both options depend for their existence on groups and institutions built around goals and practices that people share together. To choose to become an architect is to choose to join an existing set of groups, institutions, and practices that no one person created.

Similarly, to choose to become a soldier is to enter into the habits and dispositions and disciplines that make a soldier's life a soldier's life, rather than that of an artist or poet. Those habits and dispositions and disciplines are shaped by the traditions and commitments that the military carries forward from one generation to the next. To choose to become a soldier is to keep faith not only with one's fellow soldiers in the present but also with those who have come before and those who will come after.

The people who formed the conventions were not entirely free to choose, either. For the conventions are not in every respect contingent or arbitrary. Rather, many of the norms and practices are grounded in immutable truths about nature and, in particular, human nature. For example, it is simply the case that a person who trains to run a fast race by frequently running fast in practice will, all other things being equal, beat a person who has never lost a drop of sweat and who only experiences an elevated heart rate by playing video games and watching thrilling movies.

The laws of physics and of human anatomy and physiology are just what they are. Anyone who wants to succeed in an athletic endeavor, therefore, should conform his training to the skills and techniques that certain objective laws determine. There are better and worse ways of throwing a football in the sense that some techniques are more effective than others for throwing the football quickly, or a great distance, or at a high rate of speed. Those techniques are determined by the shape of a football and the physics of rotating objects traveling through the air. And they are different in important respects from the best way to throw a baseball.

The same is true of a choice to become a musician or a medical doctor, or a Roman Catholic or an Orthodox Jew. All of these choices involve submission to ways of being and acting that are themselves not determined by individual choice but instead by conventions and by even more fundamental, objective sources of truths such as human biology, gravity, and intrinsic rights and wrongs. To make meaningful choices, one must have meaningful options. Meaningful options require individuals to submit to the norms and practices of groups and communities of people.

In other words, the possibility of many valuable choices depends upon existing institutions and practices that other people built together in community, collaborating with existing nature. One who chooses such a valuable option becomes responsible for cultivating and preserving it for those who will come after. If everyone were free to decide for himself what it means to be a soldier or an athlete or an architect, then there would be no identifiable, meaningful option of a soldier's or architect's or athlete's life to choose.

To sum up, free choice is really important. To realize our potential as rational agents, we must be free of coercion, and we must have valuable options from which to choose. The capacity to author our own lives is an essential part of what makes us uniquely human.

Nevertheless, moral truth cannot be free choice all the way down. To be meaningful, an individual's free choices must eliminate at least some future choices. And to be valuable, they must conform to patterns and ways of acting that other people and communities have shaped for the person choosing. The power to choose and make new obligations for oneself is an important moral truth. But it points toward other, more foundational sources of truth that are not contingent upon free choice.

Westerners, generally, and Americans, in particular, have more personal autonomy today—more freedom and more valuable options—than any people have ever enjoyed in history. The Practical Question writ large for us is this: What am I going to do with all this free choice? Will I use it merely for individual gratification, to satisfy my own desires? Or will I use it to achieve some greater good from which others can benefit? The possibility that we can use our freedom and power of choice for a greater good suggests that personal autonomy is not the only or most important good at stake in our choices.

TRUTH IS NATURAL

A final idea posits that practical truth about what we should do is objective and independent of our assents to it, like the truths discerned in physics and mathematics. This does not mean that there is only one right answer to the Practical Question, what I should do. But it does mean that there are a few things I should never be willing to do, such as raping and enslaving, and that those people who are willing to do them are wrong. It also means that there are more and less reasonable answers to other instances of the Practical Question.[4]

If at least some truth is natural, then some of our controversies have right and wrong answers, and others have more or less reasonable answers. The moral laws of human rights being what they are, it is always wrong for a nation to allow legalized slavery. And the laws of economics being what they are, independent of what we think about them, some economic policies are objectively better than others and other economic policies are objectively worse at making us all more prosperous.

This idea is that we should do what is good for human beings and that what is good is shaped and even somewhat determined by human nature. Like animals and nonsentient beings, humans have a nature. And we should take that nature into account when interacting with it. Our nature is (partly) a rational nature. We can choose and act for *reasons*. And this makes all the difference.

We begin to understand what is right to do when we consider what is good and what is bad for human beings to choose and pursue. For example, having seen that all practical inquiry presupposes some truth, we can perceive that knowledge of the truth is good to have and is worth pursuing. Knowledge is a reason for our choices and actions. Knowledge is objectively better than ignorance. That is another way to say that ignorance is bad. Someone who prefers ignorance to knowledge is mistaken about what is to be pursued and done.

We can then reflect on what this means for our choices and actions. And we see that knowledge is good not only for me to pursue, but also for you to pursue, and for everyone else. And if we are all better off for having acquired knowledge, then we should pursue knowledge. And if we should pursue knowledge, then we should do what we can to avoid ignorance, confusion, deceit, and other less desirable conditions that prevent us from knowing what is true.

What is true of the particular good of knowledge is also true of human goods generally. In the words of the natural law philosopher Thomas Aquinas, good is to be done, and evil is to be avoided. This is true for everyone. Everyone should do what is good and should avoid intentionally doing what is evil. And this is true no matter what good is at stake, whether knowledge, friendship, health, or something else that is valuable for its own sake.

This idea of objective reasons—what is often called "natural law"—provides a comprehensive account of our moral reasoning. It explains our pluralism—why we think people can reasonably pursue different goals and life plans—and our moral imperatives—why we think some actions should never be done (at least not intentionally). Not everyone pursues the same goods, and not everyone who pursues the same goods pursues them in the same way or the same particular instance. Some people—teachers and scholars—devote themselves to a life pursuing and imparting knowledge. That is good. Others—doctors and nurses—pursue and impart health. And that is good also. There is no one right answer to the Practical Question for everyone.

Yet natural law also accounts for what is universally right and wrong. None of us should deliberately harm the good efforts and fruits of others. None of us should, for example, thwart the teacher's efforts to impart knowledge by teaching falsehoods to her students. Nor should we cause her students to doubt her veracity by defaming her, for example, by falsely accusing her of teaching falsehoods. Those actions are not right. They harm the good of the teacher and her students by thwarting their efforts to acquire knowledge. Therefore, they deprive the teacher and students of their rights.

It is always wrong to kill an innocent person on purpose, which is to destroy their life. It is always wrong to cut or slice their body for the purpose of maiming, which is to destroy their health and bodily integrity. It is always wrong to assert ownership over another person, which is to destroy their moral agency, freedom, and practical reasonableness.

Similarly, it is always wrong to communicate falsehoods that reflect badly on another person, which is to destroy their reputation and the possibility of friendship. It is always wrong to lie or cheat on an examination, which is to destroy the good of knowledge and the possibility of equal status and respect under the law of the community. To lie or cheat is to deprive a person of knowledge of the truth. And it is to usurp the rights and status of those who act honestly and who obey the rules. For these reasons, we can perceive the basic moral requirements of academic life, our exceptionless duties not to defame, lie, or cheat, and the absolute rights that other members of our academic communities have not to be defamed, lied to, or cheated against.

This line of thought leads to the conclusion that *the right thing to do is to honor and give every person his or her natural rights.* Natural rights are those rights and liberties that each and every person has simply by virtue of being a human being and possessing a human nature that is perfected in pursuit of human goods. And we can know natural rights through the exercise of reason. They are evident to those who reflect on what it means to be human.

This is the sense of the claim in the prologue of the American Declaration of Independence that we all know what rights each and every person has by "the laws of nature and nature's God." The Declaration proclaims, "We hold these truths to be self-evident, that all men are created equal, that they are endowed by their Creator with certain unalienable Rights, that among these are Life, Liberty and the pursuit of Happiness." To a reasonable mind, the duties that we all each have are evident, and therefore, the rights that correlate with those duties are also evident.

This does not mean that everyone acknowledges all natural rights. Slave owners, traffickers, and tyrants deny the authority of natural law today, just as they did in 1776. But they are being unreasonable. To a rational mind not clouded by selfish ambition and vain conceits, the natural rights of all human beings are evident. That is the idea.

Different people use different terms to refer to the rights derived from natural law. Sometimes they are called natural rights, at other times fundamental or human rights. The basic idea or assumption underlying these different expressions is that the right thing to do is out there to be discovered. The right is fixed by nature and ascertainable by reason, rather than something to be created by our individual choices or societal conventions. It exists independently of our opinions and group decisions.

This idea has a distinguished pedigree in our civic and political discourse. Civil rights leaders such as Martin Luther King Jr. appealed to the idea that natural law is higher and more authoritative than human law, and that because we can reason about what natural law guides us to do and requires us not to do, we can know when our human laws are unjust, as laws mandating racial segregation were manifestly unjust. Similarly, those who advocated for the abolition of slavery in the nineteenth century, and those who opposed its institution in law in the eighteenth century invoked the authority of natural rights and natural law.

This is also why we can have international human rights and prosecutions for their infringement. The trials of Nazi war criminals at Nuremberg were predicated on the idea that what the Nazis did was inherently wrong. The Nazis acted contrary to the rights of those whom they killed and oppressed, and this is apparent to anyone who views the evidence of their atrocities dispassionately and reasonably.

Natural law and natural rights are obviously attractive to minority groups, especially those who find themselves oppressed by tyrannical majorities. But the idea also appeals to many powerful people throughout history. Indeed, until very recently in our history, almost everyone took it for granted that there is a natural law and that it determines certain natural rights and that we should respect those rights.

For example, all of the great jurists and legal scholars from Justinian in the sixth century right through Harvard law professor and US Supreme Court Justice Joseph Story in the 1800s taught that human laws are just when they are correctly derived from natural law. Today, jurists who ascribe to the teachings of natural law include Oxford philosopher John Finnis, Princeton philosopher Robert P. George, as well as the religion scholar Rabbi David Novak. Natural law is not a fringe idea. Our laws were built on its foundation, and it continues to run straight down the middle of our intellectual heritage.

Now, we must hasten to observe that human laws and civil rights are not all derived in the same way from natural law and natural rights. Some are derived more directly than others. At least some natural rights are absolute and immutable, and therefore not contingent upon individual choice or the conventions of groups and societies. These are derived directly from natural law. For example, it is always wrong to kill an innocent person on purpose, because each and every human being has a natural right to life. And that is because human life is good in itself. The value of human life is not contingent upon our choice of it, nor upon life's instrumental value to realize other goods. Therefore, it is always wrong to kill an innocent person intentionally.

However, most natural rights are contingent and context-dependent, because they are derived from natural law not directly but indirectly, and require some specification according to circumstance. For example, we have a general obligation to educate our young people. But how to satisfy that obligation must necessarily vary according to our circumstances. How much education? What kind: liberal, vocational, technical? Who pays? For how long? What if resources run short, or they must be spent satisfying some other need? The right to receive an education is contingent on all these variables and more.

This is not to deny that knowledge is valuable. It is always wrong to lie or defame, in part because those actions destroy knowledge of the truth. And people have rights not to be defamed or lied to because we all have duties not to lie or defame. Notice again that our absolute duties, which correlate with absolute rights, are all duties of abstention—duties to refrain from acting in some way. By contrast, obligations of action, such as our obligation to educate our children, necessarily vary according to context. So, rights to receive something or to require someone to do something for us cannot be absolute. They are inherently contingent and defeasible.

The idea of natural law thus provides the most promising place to look for comprehensive, moral truth. Natural law teaches us those actions that we must never intentionally do, and thus yields absolute, fundamental rights. And it teaches us how to think about our sources of reasonable disagreement. It leaves room for both conventional norms and free choices, while also marking off the boundaries of those moral domains.

NOTES

1. The technical, philosophical term for this is operational (or performative) self-refutation. The act of denying the existence of truth refutes the claim that there is no truth. The philosopher John Finnis gives the examples, "No one can put words (or other symbols) together to form a sentence," and "I do not exist." To state in a sentence that no one can form a sentence is to refute the very statement contained in the sentence. To assert that one does not exist is to demonstrate one's existence. An operationally self-refuting statement "is inevitably falsified by an assertion of it." John Finnis, *Natural Law and Natural Rights*, 74 (2nd ed., Oxford: Oxford University Press, 2011).

2. Joseph Raz, *The Morality of Freedom*, 369–78 (Oxford: Oxford University Press, 1986).

3. Raz at 380; Robert P. George, *Making Men Moral*, 173–82 (Oxford: Oxford University Press, 1993).

4. Much of what follows draws heavily from classical moral and jurisprudential theory, especially Thomas Aquinas, Summa Theologica I-II Questions 90–108 (the part of the *Summa* known as the "Treatise on Law"), and John Finnis, *Natural Law and Natural Rights* (2nd ed., Oxford: Oxford University Press, 2011).

SEVEN

Should and Must Not

SELFIE CULTURE AND THE CHALLENGES OF GOVERNANCE

Now we broaden our perspective. In the first six chapters, we focused on the immediate and personal. It is important to understand that discourse about our most controversial questions is first and foremost practical discourse about real persons. The Practical Question concerns my actions and your actions. We must first grasp the concreteness and immediacy of our moral inquiries if we are to make any progress in reasoning together about what is to be done. As we have seen, the question, "What is right?", is not (just) an abstract question but a practical one.

Having paid close attention to the first-person perspective on our discourse, we are now in a position to move up a level and consider what is right for *us* to do—not just you and me as individuals but also us together as communities of people working together to achieve common goods. Here again, the way we are engaging in discourse presently poses an obstacle. To the extent that our discourse is about our personal identities, our individual rights, and the ways other people wrong us, we will not get very far in thinking about the common good that we all share. And we will not be able to answer the question of what is right for us to do together.

The selfie way of thinking generates challenges not only for young people but also for the rest of us, for everyone. We need to understand two such challenges in particular. First, it is not clear whether this new, identity-based conception of right and wrong is compatible with the rule of law and civic order. Indeed, there are reasons to think that we cannot have both a selfie culture and a culture that respects the rule of law. Second, to the extent that each person's moral references are entirely internal to that person, it is not clear that any of us can reason together with anyone else about what is right and wrong. If what is right is entirely subjective and constituted by personal identity, then we have no inherent reasons to take other people's sense of right and wrong into account.

To see these challenges clearly, consider a true story related by a student. The story concerns a conflict that the student experienced with the president of his undergraduate college. It illustrates well how different generations think about moral questions. And it neatly frames the challenges that we will face as the younger generations come of age and exercise more power and responsibility in public life.

The student who related the story is of mixed race. One of his races is Native American. To celebrate his native identity, he wanted to wear a ceremonial feather on his cap at commencement exercises. College administrators told him that this was not allowed. College rules prohibit decorations on graduation regalia. The college refused to allow an exception for this student. The stated purposes of the rules are to preserve a uniform appearance among members of the graduating class and to avoid distracting symbols and statements that might detract from the occasion. To allow an exception for one student would, in justice, require allowing many students to disregard the rule. And that would defeat the purposes of the rule.

The student pressed the issue all the way to the college president's office. As the student later related, the president explained that the rule "applies to everyone else." The student "wasn't being singled out." However, the student was not interested in being treated the same as everyone else. When the president did not relent, the student threatened to contact news media outlets and take his dissatisfaction public. At this threat, the president relented, and the student wore his feather as he graduated.

This story illustrates a significant generational difference. Each man thought he was doing what was right. The student wanted to wear a symbol of his personal identity. He did not intend to harm or offend anyone. He was, in his own judgment, not doing anything wrong. In his own words, wearing the feather made him feel good. "I enjoyed it," he later recounted. It was a way to manifest his cultural heritage and celebrate what he had achieved.

The feather was also intended to communicate a moral message. The student related that some of his family members live in poverty on a Native American reservation and that he identifies their plight with America's moral failings. When considering whether to wear the feather, the student thought of "strong figures in history" who had engaged in civil disobedience. He sought to follow their example. He later explained:

> I really wanted to wear the ceremonial feather as many of my family members have worn it upon their graduations. The rule the school had made sense to me, but not in this instance. I can understand why the school wanted uniformity, but I didn't see how my ceremonial

feather would be a distraction. I thought of all the pain and turmoil my ancestors went through. I looked at how the school is built on what used to be my tribe's land. Upon reflection, it was easy to see that the rule was too restrictive, and it needed to be updated for instances like mine.

Meanwhile, the president was not doing anything wrong. He was not discriminating against the student. On the contrary, he was applying the same rule to the student that he applied to everyone else. Presumably, in his own judgment, the president was doing what was right and just. As president, he had a duty to enforce the rules as written, uniformly, without giving special preference to one student. To make an exception only in one case would be unjust to other students.

This story illustrates the challenges that we will face in the near future as young people educated in the morality of personal identity come to occupy more places and play a larger role in society. In itself, the disagreement was not significant. The student and the president had a minor conflict over a small token of personal identity. The student was calm, respectful, and thoughtful as he related the story, nothing like the rabid student protestors whose images now command so much media attention. Indeed, he is a diligent, intelligent, and responsible young man.

Nevertheless, as an example of the thinking of young people, the student's reasoning portends a significant challenge to the rule of law, ordered liberty, and equal protection of the laws. And it suggests that we will increasingly find it difficult to reason together on the basis of objective principles and norms.

The student was not willing to submit to the rules of the college that he had chosen to attend. He formed his own judgment about the reasons for the college's rule requiring uniformity of commencement regalia and concluded that it should not apply to him. The judgment was his alone, and it was predicated on opinions that are his alone. And he is not an isolated example. His views about rules, authority, and reason are widely shared by other members of his generation. The implications of his attitude are not hard to perceive. If everyone is free to judge for themselves whether the uniform general rules should be applied to them and to decide whether to obey the rules, then we cannot have a society governed by rules. Nor can we have reasoned discourse.

When relating this story, the student said that he had drawn inspiration for his actions from conscientious dissenters of earlier times who had disobeyed rules and edicts they thought were unjust. Law students at the law school where I teach read about and consider several examples of such dissenters, both fictional and real. Antigone in the play by Sophocles, Socrates in Plato's account of the trial and death of his teacher, Saint Paul in the Christian scriptures, and Martin Luther King Jr. sitting in a Birmingham Jail all appealed to a law higher than human law—the law of God or of the gods, or the law of nature. When confronted with human laws that conflicted directly with the higher law, they all chose to obey the higher law.

My student differs from those earlier examples of conscientious dissent in two important respects. First, each of the earlier conscientious dissenters acted with knowledge of the legal consequences for their actions and willingly accepted those consequences. This is what made them heroic. Antigone, Socrates, Saint Paul, and Martin Luther King Jr. all were jailed or imprisoned for their conscientious disobedience, and three of them died in prison. Socrates taught that it would be unjust for him to flee Athens and avoid his death sentence because he had spent his life in Athens enjoying the benefits of the same laws under which he was now (unjustly) condemned. And Paul and King both taught that a conscientious objector also *must* be willing to accept legal consequences such as imprisonment for conscientious disobedience to the law.

By contrast, this student sought to avoid the consequences of his decision to break the rules. Indeed, the point of his conversations with the college president was to secure the benefits of not following the rules while avoiding undesirable consequences. Rather than demonstrate his conviction by bearing the cost of his decision, he increased the cost of enforcement by threatening to attract the attention of local media. Of course, that tipped the balance of power in the student's favor, for the president's (valid and nondiscriminatory) reasons for enforcing the rules would have been submerged beneath charges of insensitivity toward racial minorities, or perhaps even bigotry.

Second, each of the earlier exemplars of conscientious dissent appealed to a law higher than human law—the law of God, the law of reason, or natural justice. Conscientious dissenters throughout history have not all invoked their own rights. Many of the most influential have instead invoked their moral duties and obligations. They have understood themselves to be morally obligated both to human rulers and to God or some higher law. They believed that they had an obligation both to disobey civil authorities and to submit to civil authorities. They were obligated to disobey human law because it conflicted with a higher law, and they were likewise obligated to accept the consequences of their disobedience because they enjoyed the benefits of living under the law. They were not champions of anarchy but rather of obedience to law, even as they sought to change the law for everyone (instead of seeking special exemptions for themselves).

Unlike the student, who felt obliged to disobey the rules to maintain integrity with his own identity—his internal standard of right—Antigone, Paul, and King all said that they were obligated to obey God even if that meant disobeying human rulers. Similarly, Socrates chose to remain faithful to the dictates of reason and justice. They all looked for guidance, not inside themselves but rather outside and above themselves. In considering and choosing what to do, they referred to norms or ideals that they understood to be open for examination by, and morally binding on, everyone. Others might disagree with their judgments. But they could recognize the *reasons* for disagreement.

LAW FOR US

As this example illustrates, the selfie culture poses a dichotomy. It demands that we choose between lawfulness and personal fulfillment. To follow the rules blindly is to be untrue to oneself. From this perspective, officials who enforce the rules without regard to personal identity are acting like tyrants. On the other hand, if everyone disregards the rules and does what is right in his own eyes, then we court chaos and anarchy. If we make particular, individual exceptions for some, then we must in justice make individual exceptions for others. At some point, a dozen, or a hundred, or a thousand exceptions swallow the rule.

Fortunately, the dichotomy is false, as we see from the examples of Antigone, Socrates, Saint Paul, and Martin Luther King Jr. We need not choose between tyranny and anarchy. We need not all obey the law blindly, no matter how unjust, and we need not allow every person to be a law unto himself. We can have the rule of law, *and* we can critique unjust laws on grounds of reason. We can reason together about what is right for us to do.

We go wrong if we allow every person to decide for themselves what to do. We need to act together to achieve our good ends. Therefore, we need general rules and particular obligations. For a college to pursue the good of knowledge, the faculty, staff, and students must coordinate their actions. This does not mean that everyone must be the same or act the same. On the contrary, justice requires that we allow differences to flourish (as we will see later). However, members of the community must have duties and must honor them. And the members of the community can and should recognize those duties in reason, not (just) because someone in authority told them so but because they know (or should know) that it is right.

Those who make and enforce the rules and those who are governed by them must alike be governed by law. Indeed, the entire community should be lawful. Faculty must communicate their expectations clearly (for example, in a syllabus), show up for class, lead or coordinate the class discussion, and grade (if at all) on the basis of standards that apply equally to everyone and are promulgated in advance. Students must respect the expertise of their teachers and the efforts of their classmates by not talking out of turn, performing the assignments, and refraining from personal attacks and other expressions that destroy the learning environment. The administration must enforce the rules equally and justly. All of these general obligations and particular duties conduce to the common good of acquiring and disseminating knowledge, which is the college's purpose. In short, the college could not be a college without these sources of obligation.

For the same reason, we do not need the most powerful person to tell us what is to be done and not done. We can avoid tyranny. We can know and do what is right and wrong to do—we can make law to govern ourselves, and we can live under that law—without the sovereign telling us what the law will be. We can be lawful even without a law promulgated by the political sovereign. Therefore, we can be lawful even without first achieving a political consensus. We can do what is right together for the same reason that we can do right individually. We can reason.

The reason we can know what is right to do is that we know basic human rights. We know human rights because we know basic human duties. And we know our duties because we know what is good. By acting to realize good ends, we incur duties toward other people, who share the good with us. And, as we saw earlier, the flip side of a right is someone's duty. Our duties toward other people just are their rights. To secure those rights, which secure our duties, which secure the common good, we make law.

At the very least, we can know absolute human rights, because we know that certain actions are intrinsically wrong. In general, we all know that we have exceptionless duties not to cause certain harm to others intentionally—duties not to kill, maim, rape, and enslave. Each of those actions injures a person in a basic aspect of their well-being, and so it is never to be done intentionally.

Notice that each of those absolute duties correlates with another person's absolute right—rights not to be killed, maimed, raped, and enslaved. And because each of those duties is a duty of abstention—a duty to do nothing—we can extend the duty to our interactions with every other person in exactly the same way and all the time, whatever the circumstances and resources at hand. Unlike an affirmative obligation to feed a person, for example, which is contingent upon there being food to offer, upon the person being in need of food, and upon our prior duties to feed our own families and those under our care (among other variables), duties not to do intentional wrongs are not contingent and particular but absolute and universal. Thus, the correlative rights are universal and absolute rights.

Now things get a bit more complicated. That we can say with confidence what few acts *we must not do* does not entail that we can all agree what acts *we should do*. Consider the obligation to feed people. That obligation is contingent and variable, not absolute and universal. One has the obligation only if one has food to offer, and then perhaps only upon payment of a fair price by those who are able to pay, so that those who grew, produced, and served the food can be justly compensated for their investments of time and resources. The obligation varies according to the resources available. It is specified differently in a rural village where only rice and beans are available than at a state dinner where heads of state will gather to broker a peace deal that might secure peace and prosperity for millions of people. The obligation also varies according to the relationships at issue and the prior obligations between them. For example, one has a prior obligation to feed one's own children before attempting to feed someone else's children.

Nevertheless, we can reason our way to many non-absolute rights and duties. Indeed, we can deduce most of the rules, rights, and duties that coordinate and order our daily interactions, either directly from natural law or from our customs and conventions that specify the requirements of natural law. In fact, we *do* reason to correct conclusions about what we owe each other and how to treat each other. We do it all the time. Most of the time, we do it without any awareness that we are doing it. Whether or not we stop to reflect on our own reasoning, each of us daily practices natural law as we go about reasoning what to do and not do with respect to other people.

Recall again the example of walking through a parking lot full of automobiles. As you pass row after row of cars and trucks searching for your own, you know what you are (not) to do with respect to the automobiles you pass. You know that you should not enter or take them. You have a duty to exclude yourself from them. You don't need to know who owns the cars, or what the owners plan to do with them, or whether you might come up with a better plan for their use. And you don't need anyone to tell you what is to be done. You know. And so you exclude yourself from the cars.

Your duty to exclude yourself from the cars rests on important moral considerations. For example, people often work hard to earn money to buy their cars, and it would be unjust to deprive them of the fruits of their labor by taking their cars. Also, people make plans for the use and maintenance of their cars. To interfere with their plans by taking the car, or to disrespect their right to decide how the car is to be used by entering the car without permission, is to disrespect the owner or lawful possessor as a human being, a maker of good plans for the things under their authority and control.

Here again, by focusing on the duties we owe to each other and the good reasons for those duties, we can reason our way to the rights we owe each other. You owe to each and every owner of each and every car in that parking lot a duty not to enter or take their cars. Arising out of and correlating with your duty toward each owner is the owner's right to exclude you from their car. This property right, the right to exclude, is a foundational right in our law. It is entailed in what we owe each other. And we can know it through the exercise of reason.

Property rights are not absolute. They differ slightly from the rights not to be enslaved or defamed. Yet we can know property rights, such as the right to exclude, through the exercise of reason because it admits of just a few, narrow exceptions. And we all know the exceptions by reason, even if we've never been to law school. Imagine that, as you walk through the parking lot, you see a child trapped in one of the cars. The temperature is very high, and the child appears to be listless, bright red, and in distress—signs of heatstroke. At that moment, you have no duty to exclude yourself from the car. Instead, you have a right to break into the car to rescue the child.

The law ratifies this reasoning in a rule known as the "necessity doctrine." As every first-year law student learns, the doctrine teaches that the nonowner has no duty of self-exclusion when entry is strictly necessary to save someone's life. This doctrine and the right to life that it secures also form a foundational aspect of our law.

The reason for the necessity doctrine is obvious. A human life is valuable in and of itself. It is, in the words of moral philosophers, "a basic human good." Therefore, no reasoned plan can be *more* important than saving a human life. Whatever the owner of the car had intended to do or not do with the car, we can say with certainty that no reasonable owner would want you to exclude yourself from the car if entering the car is the necessary means to save a child's life. Therefore, the law imputes a reasonable intention both to the rescuer and to the owner and concludes that the owner had no right to exclude in this case.

Notice that the doctrine of necessity is not a general license to enter other people's land or things without permission. Only a few very basic and important categories of reasons will suffice to justify an unconsented entry. Saving a human life counts. So does serving due process to bring a legal wrongdoer to justice. However, nearly every other reason you might have for entering or using a thing that belongs to someone else without their permission will not suffice, even if it's a very good reason, and even if it's a better reason than the owner's reason for excluding you. Indeed, the owner owes you no explanation for excluding you. This is what makes private property such an important countermajoritarian institution in a free society. It is why all the great civil rights movements have been birthed behind closed doors on private property, and it is why private ownership is such an important defense of the weak and vulnerable against the rich and powerful.

Intellectual property rights have the same structure for similar reasons. Basic human goods justify rights of exclusive use in intellectual creations. The good of knowledge is both instrumental and intrinsic, and it grounds duties not to misappropriate others' intellectual creations. Out of those duties and correlating with them arise intellectual property rights in inventions (i.e., trade secrets and patents), expressions (i.e., copyrights), and business goodwill (i.e., trademarks).

Moreover, precisely because the good of knowledge is not merely basic but also intrinsic, the law recognizes inherent limitations on intellectual property rights, such as the rights of nonowners to make fair uses of copyrighted expressions and to use patented inventions for purely educational purposes. Because our duties just are the rights of others (and vice versa), the owner of a copyright has no claim against one making a fair use, and the owner of a patent has no claim against one who makes a purely experimental or philosophical use. Both of those limitations on intellectual property rights secure the good of knowledge. Fair use and experimental use are inherent limitations on intellectual property rights to secure a real human good, just as the necessity to save a human life is an inherent limitation on property rights in tangible assets and resources.

RESPONSIBILITY FOR KNOWING AND MAKING LAW

Because we know what is good and bad, right and wrong to do, we can reason together about what is good and right for us to do. And we can make law for ourselves so that we can avoid doing what is wrong. The human capacity for practical reason enables each of us to be a lawful creature—full of the law and responsive to it in our choices and actions. And this is true not only regarding our obligations not to kill, enslave, steal, and infringe but also with respect to less determinate obligations. Especially in democracies and democratic republics, where we the people enjoy the power to make our public laws, we all bear a responsibility to reason well about what the law should be. And everywhere, people bear a responsibility to make their private obligations reasonable—to choose and act in their conveyances, contracts, and other acts of private ordering for what is good and right.

We need private law just as much as we need public law. As we have seen, most of the natural law does not consist of determinate rights and duties and exceptionless norms. Very few natural rights are absolute. Most natural law falls into that category of less determinate reason. Jurists in the Continental European tradition and nations that inherited their law from the Continent, such as those in South America, follow the medieval philosopher Thomas Aquinas in calling this area of law *determinatio* or "determinations." Jurists in the English common law tradition and nations that inherited their laws from England, such as the United States and Australia, follow Aristotle in calling these indeterminate legal questions "matters of indifference." Both terms refer to roughly the same idea. In these matters, natural law supplies general principles that establish presumptions and guide practical reasoning but leaves most of the specification of natural duties to persons and groups of persons.

Consider, for example, the obligation that parents have to nourish, nurture, and educate their children. This general obligation can reasonably be specified in any number of ways. Indeed, it *should* be specified differently for different children, even within the same family. The education of an athletic child should, in justice, consist of different instruction than that given to the musical child. The child with allergies should have a different diet than one without. Different parents have different resources and opportunities available to them. And children are not the only persons who make just demands on the parents' time and resources, and so on. Therefore, there is great freedom to choose and act according to circumstance and judgment—there is no one right way to raise children.

And yet, no one doubts that a child has a right to her parent's care and instruction and that parents who have the means and nevertheless fail to supply what their children need have violated their children's rights. This is why states are justified in taking custody of children in cases of abuse and extreme neglect. Parents must be free to decide how best to raise their children and are entitled to a strong presumption of custodial and parental rights. But the political community can hold the parents accountable to fulfill their responsibilities until the child is old enough to act on her own behalf, and in extreme cases of abuse, well-proven on competent evidence, the state might have the power (against the parents) and duty (to the child) to remove abused children from their natural parents and attempt to place them in the custody of persons who will care for them.

Similarly, college professors and administrators have a general obligation to educate their students. This general obligation gives rise to the presumption that they are, in fact, educating their students and that they should be free to decide precisely how to do the job. This is why educational pluralism is a good thing. Not every college must follow the same practices or rules or impose the same duties on its members. (We will return to this idea in the last chapter.) And yet, no one doubts that a college whose graduates had not learned anything during their time on campus, or who had learned vices and attitudes incompatible with knowledge of truth and with civil discourse, would have failed to meet its most basic and profound obligations.

To sum up: *What we must not do is absolute and universal; what we should do is contingent and variable.* We can reason together about both questions but in different ways. A just and reasonable community, whether a family, a college, a state, or a nation, should attend to this distinction. The members of the community must stand ready to secure (the few) absolute rights that correlate with exceptionless duties *and* should allow some freedom to specify matters of indifference, those affirmative claims and entitlements that correlate with affirmative obligations, which are contingent upon the goods being pursued and other circumstances.

OBLIGATION TO OBEY LAW AND TO CHANGE LAW

This does not mean that everyone should be free to make their own laws in matters of indifference. As Socrates, Saint Paul, Martin Luther King Jr., and other conscientious leaders observed, we all have an obligation in justice to obey the law. And this obligation sometimes persists even when we have personally been treated unjustly. It always pertains when the law is reasonable and not unjust. As long as those in authority have exercised their authority lawfully and have not specified the law in direct conflict with fundamental rights and duties, obedience to the law is our moral obligation.

We need law in order to secure absolute rights. Some people stand ready to defame and cheat, even to enslave and kill. They must be restrained by lawful means. And we need law in order to settle matters of *determinatio* or indifference. Precisely because reasonable minds can disagree, and because we need to know what should be done, we need a lawful means to settle such questions conclusively. Once the law has settled these questions, we all have an obligation to obey the law. For example, once the law specifies that everyone should drive on the right side of the road, we all have an obligation to drive on the right side of the road.

This is particularly true where we have our choice of communities. Socrates thought it would be unjust to flee Athens after his conviction in part because he had been free to leave Athens earlier and had chosen to stay. The customs and laws of Athens made life in Athens pleasant and conducive to his line of work, which was speaking and reasoning freely about practical questions. He could have gone elsewhere but benefited from staying. It would be unjust to accept the benefits of Athenian law without accepting the cost.

Similarly, young people today have many options when it comes to choosing a college or university. If someone chooses to attend a college because its customs and rules are conducive to their education and advantageous to them personally, then they have chosen to accept the benefits of the college's customs and rules. Having made that choice, to usurp the college's customs and rules which are not personally advantageous is like taking something without paying for it. It is a kind of stealing.

This is a hard teaching. Who today can accept it? We act daily under a standing temptation to obey only those laws that we deem personally just and beneficial. And yet we do not hesitate to appropriate the benefits of living under law.

This is not to suggest that we should be silent in the face of injustice. Sometimes laws must be changed because they are directly contrary to reason and in conflict with absolute rights. Other laws might not be unjust in substance but were enacted illicitly, by corrupt means or without lawful authority. We might have an affirmative obligation to advocate against those laws.

Nevertheless, we should be cautious when advocating for legal change. For one thing, we should be confident that the proposal for which we advocate would not be worse than the status quo. We should ensure that the new proposal is not also inherently unjust. And we should think carefully about side effects and consequences, intended and unintended, that the new proposal is likely to bring about.

Also, changing the law sometimes undermines (both illegitimate and legitimate) customs and expectations. When people order their lives in reliance upon the law and then the law changes suddenly and radically, their affairs can be disrupted, or even thrown into turmoil. This generates costs for everyone. Consider a simple and dramatic example. Imagine a nation where people drive on the right side of the road, and a national legislature changes the law to require everyone immediately to be driving on the left. Consider not only the habits and disciplines of driving that will need to be relearned, the likelihood of accidents as people change their habits unequally and irregularly, but also all the vehicle designs that will need to be reengineered to place driving controls on the right side of automobiles, the number of years it will take before most, much less all, of the vehicles on the road are configured correctly, the massive reordering of signs and lights, intersection exchanges, curb breaks and entrances to businesses and residences, and all the other changes that states and citizens will need to make before traffic flows smoothly again.

Legal change is not only difficult but also generally unwise unless grounded in really important reasons. The more ancient the status quo, the more important and fundamental the reasons required to justify changing it. Absolute rights are always sufficient. For example, justice required legislatures to abolish the slave trade even though whole industries had grown up in reliance upon its legal status because it can never be reasonable to enslave another human being. The creation of the slave trade in British, Portuguese, and Spanish colonies in the New World in the sixteenth through nineteenth centuries was inherently unjust, and its abolition was not only justified but required as a matter of reason.

By contrast, we ought to be cautious before using the law to abolish customs and defeat expectations that are not inherently unjust. Most of our present controversies fall into this category. Suppose, for example, that most people think that education finance should be reformed. Imagine that we conclude that the current laws, under which the national government subsidizes student loans for college and university students, generates financial incentives for colleges and universities to inflate tuition prices and other charges, and induces students to incur unsustainable debt. We want to change the law, and we have good reasons to do so. But we should proceed with caution.

The current laws are not infringing upon anyone's absolute rights. They certainly impose burdens on young people. And those burdens are not equal to the burdens incurred by their parents and grandparents to receive a comparable education. So, we might conclude that the laws are unjust and should be changed. But we should first do no harm. We should not change the law if the new law will make the problem worse, or if it will generate new problems that are more onerous, or if it will harm the very educational institutions that impart knowledge in the first place. Nor should we be keen to change the law retrospectively. Debts and obligations already contracted and incurred should be respected and enforced unless inherently exploitative or otherwise contrary to fundamental rights, both because people have an obligation to keep their promises and because widespread default would drive up costs for everyone.

In other words, it is complicated. Most of our political and legal controversies are. Moral principles alone do not always, or even often, resolve the question of what should be done. This is not to deny that some of our controversies are moral all the way down. The legality of abortion is an obvious example of a controversy about fundamental rights. Pro-lifers and abortion rights supporters do not agree on much, but they both think that the issue is not as complicated as education finance. And they are correct. If the mother has a fundamental right to obtain an abortion and the doctor has a fundamental immunity for performing one, then we do not need to consider the likely side effects of abortion laws or other prudential considerations; the law should not prohibit abortion. On the other hand, if the unborn child has a fundamental right to life, then the law should prohibit abortion. There is no complicated middle ground.

However, most issues are more complicated than abortion. And even on thoroughly moral issues such as abortion, we should hesitate to assume that there is only one just solution. There is principled room for compromise in working out the law's remedy for infringements of fundamental rights. For example, pro-lifers think that abortion prohibitions should apply to abortionists rather than mothers. And there remain further questions about what sanctions and remedies the law should specify for disobeying those prohibitions: whether criminal sanctions or civil liability or professional censure is the most appropriate response, how long and how much to punish or hold liable, and so forth.

Reflecting on this distinction between what we must not do (i.e., absolute rights and duties) and what we should do (i.e., matters of *determinatio* or indifference) should lead us to greater humility in our moral discourse. We might all recognize in ourselves a temptation to do things we must not do, such as defame other people or lie about them. And we might recognize that on many controversial questions, there is room for reasonable people to disagree. These realizations might motivate us to assert moral claims with more grace and openness to countervailing considerations. They might also motivate us to defend truly absolute rights with greater conviction. In short, we might go about the business of moral discourse with greater clarity and charity. And we should recognize the indispensable role of law in making our communities good places to live together.

EIGHT

The "S" Word

That moral judgment is possible means that it is possible for us to do wrong. And none of us is immune. We are all human. And humans are flawed. The classical tradition has a word for this reality. It's not a nice word, and many people think this word should not be said in polite company. But our refusal to use this word only prevents us from acknowledging the ways that we each contribute to the incivility of our public discourse and makes us less understanding of the failures of others.

In the language of the Hebrew and Christian traditions, we all "sin." Sin is an ancient idea that explains what we see around us today. Moreover, it can help us to reason together with greater civility and hope of seeing together what is right to do. The recognition that we all sin enables us to see each other as equals. Even when we disagree, and even when our opponents espouse views that we find morally abhorrent, we can see in other people beings who are good by design but corrupted by wrong thinking and actions. And we can see the same thing in ourselves.

Aleksandr Solzhenitsyn, a war hero of the Russian campaign against Nazi Germany and unjustly convicted prisoner of Stalin's gulags, memorably expressed this truth in his work *The Gulag Archipelago*. It would be easy to rid ourselves of wrongdoing, he observed, if we could simply identify all the wrongdoers, separate them from society, and then destroy them. "But the line dividing good and evil cuts through the heart of every human being."

This idea has helped Americans to heal from deep and violent divisions in our history. As the American Civil War drew to a close, President Lincoln was sworn into office for a second time. On that day, March 4, 1865, he delivered what some people think was his greatest speech. (It is now chiseled on an inside wall within the Lincoln Memorial in Washington, DC.) In his Second Inaugural Address, Lincoln pleaded with his "fellow-countrymen," Northerners and Southerners, Unionists and rebels, abolitionists and slave owners—the American people—to acknowledge their mutual complicity in slavery and to extend friendship to each other in humility.

One side went to war to destroy the Union. The other accepted war to preserve it, Lincoln insisted. Yet both sides knew that slavery "was somehow the cause of the war." True, slaves were "not distributed generally over the Union, but localized in the southern part of it." And to Lincoln and other Northerners, the idea that the Union should be dissolved to preserve slavery was not only unpersuasive but incomprehensible. "It may seem strange that any men should dare to ask a just God's assistance in wringing their bread from the sweat of other men's faces." But slavery came into the Union by the actions and omissions of Southerners and Northerners alike. And so, God was just to exact punishment against both. Quoting the Bible—the same authority to which both abolitionists and slave owners had appealed—Lincoln continued:

> The Almighty has His own purposes. "Woe unto the world because of offenses; for it must needs be that offenses come, but woe to that man by whom the offense cometh." If we shall suppose that American slavery is one of those offenses which, in the providence of God, must needs come, but which, having continued through His appointed time, He now wills to remove, and that He gives to both North and South this terrible war as the woe due to those by whom the offense came, shall we discern therein any departure from those divine attributes which the believers in a living God always ascribe to Him? Fondly do we hope, fervently do we pray, that this mighty scourge of war may speedily pass away. Yet, if God wills that it continue until all the wealth piled by the bondsman's two hundred and fifty years of unrequited toil shall be sunk, and until every drop of blood drawn with the lash shall be paid by another drawn with the sword, as was said three thousand years ago, so still it must be said "the judgments of the Lord are true and righteous altogether."[1]

Lincoln's moral assessment does not entail that all Americans were equally culpable in slavery. A slave, for one, could not be blamed for his own captivity. Many Americans worked and fought to achieve abolition. Even many of those who fought and died in service to the Confederacy had no personal stake in slavery and had other motivations for doing what they believed was their moral duty. But Lincoln understood and articulated the conviction shared by his fellow countrymen that the Almighty's purposes are far above ours. We are sinners; God alone is righteous.

This conviction motivated Lincoln to extend grace rather than to recriminate. Having set the predicate in place, Lincoln concluded with his famous admonition:

With malice toward none, with charity for all, with firmness in the right as God gives us to see the right, let us strive on to finish the work we are in, to bind up the nation's wounds, to care for him who shall have borne the battle and for his widow and his orphan, to do all which may achieve and cherish a just and lasting peace among ourselves and with all nations.

Though many people find it hard to believe now, Lincoln and his fellow countrymen believed in righteousness and sin. We are fortunate that they did. Many Americans today still do. But even if the idea of sin corresponds to no reality, it is nevertheless a useful idea. Whether or not the Hebrew or Christian tradition is correct, the idea of sin is helpful. It enables us to see clearly one way in which we truly are equal. *We all fail to do what we should, and sometimes we even do what we must not do.* This suggests that we should approach each other with humility and grace. Those virtues would soften our discourse and make it both more civil and more productive.

WHAT SIN IS NOT

The idea of sin has fallen into disfavor in part because people misunderstand it. When people hear the word "sin," they tend to think of the pre-Hebrew, pre-Christian pagan idea of sin as offenses against petulant gods and goddesses. Ancient deities were thought to issue arbitrary edicts because they craved the obedience and adoration of humans. To sin was to cause offense to a god whose own interests were at stake. That is not the idea of sin that we find in Hebrew and Christian scriptures.

The Hebrew idea of God, which Jews bequeathed to Christians, is that God is outside of time and space, all-sufficient, and the source of all that is. He calls Himself by the name "I am." He needs nothing from us. He created us out of love, a desire that we would seek friendship with Him in gratitude for the gift of existence and all the other good things in the world He entrusted to us. Far from being petulant and arbitrary, God gives rules and commands for the benefit and well-being of his creatures: Adam and Eve and their sons and daughters.

In this account, God created humans in His image. Therefore, our original nature is good. In the Genesis account, God called it "very good." Sin is the undoing of our good nature that results from rejecting God's gifts. To sin is to act contrary to our design. To offend against God's righteousness is to choose a worse state of affairs over a better one. Of course, it does not often seem like that at the time. In the moment, sinful acts often feel good, even liberating. But to judge based on our feelings in the moment is not reasonable. In the long term and in retrospect, we can often perceive that our wrong actions caused us harm, even when they did not harm others. Some of them even made us subject to bad habits and vices that we later have come to regret.

Two errors about human failure tend to prevent people from understanding and accepting this account of sin. Though these errors ultimately collapse into each other, at first glance, they appear as opposing errors, flanking the truth on each side. On one side, we find those who say that it is sinful to pursue the good things of the world for their own sake because nothing and no one is intrinsically good other than God, the ultimate summum bonum. In this view, sin is not acting contrary to our good nature or to reason. Instead, it is simply disobeying God's commands. God's commands are inscrutable, they think. And they teach that it is impious to question God. This error sometimes appears as fundamentalism or legalism, but often it appears more subtly as a simple faith, cloaked in the mantle of humble obedience.

On the other side, we find those who deny that there is anything at all significant about sin. Human nature is malleable, they say. And God, if he (or she) exists at all, is not particularly concerned about what we do with our bodies and our lives. Sure, we make mistakes. But our mistakes are just part of life. They have no inherent, enduring significance. Unless our errors result in bad consequences for others, they are not cause for regret. Religious people who cling to the idea of sin have not kept up with the times, they think. This error sometimes appears as licentiousness or hedonism, but often, it appears more subtly as an enlightened tolerance, accepting of everyone and opposed to judgmentalism.

Let us begin with legalism, the idea that it is sinful to delight in what is good. At the bottom of this view is the idea that sin consists in disobeying God's inscrutable commands. We cannot hope to understand God's reasons, for His ways are infinitely higher than our ways. And no good thing in this world can compare with the ultimate good of God's glory. His reason is perfect; ours is limited and defective. Therefore, we must accept that His commands might be arbitrary from our perspective. Indeed, that we cannot understand is the whole point. In this view, God wants us to learn to obey Him out of a recognition of His benevolence, omniscience, and sovereignty. We must learn to trust God, which means we must not interrogate His commands too rigorously.

To many people, this view of sin makes God seem like either a narcissist or a tyrant. Perhaps God cannot tolerate people who enjoy the good things He made unless those people desire Him more. Or perhaps He likes to boss people around without regard for what is good. Understandably, people tend to find this conception of God unattractive. Moreover, they find this idea of sin not very compelling. It seems that one cannot avoid offending such a god, and it does not seem worthwhile to try. This God seems not very interested in us as persons but only as subjects.

This account of God and sin is not the Jewish or Christian account. Neither the narcissist god nor the arbitrary sovereign is the God whom we meet in Hebrew and Christian scriptures. The God of the Bible delights in the inherent goodness of His creation, the independent excellence of His best creatures, and the moral agency of His people, Adam and Eve, and their sons and daughters. Throughout the creation account at the beginning of the book of Genesis, God repeatedly exclaims that the world He is creating is good, in each and every aspect.

The God of the Bible especially wants human beings to be free to love Him by cultivating and enjoying His good gifts, and He expresses happiness when we do. God tells Adam and Eve to take dominion over the world, as He exercises dominion over all of time and space. And He calls their dominion "very good." He calls Moses, Enoch, Abraham, Peter, and John the Evangelist his friends. He even brags about his favorites. "Have you considered my servant, Job?" God asks Satan. "[T]here is none like him on the earth, a blameless and upright man, who fears God and turns away from evil." In a contemporary idiom, God is saying, *Look at Job! He is awesome.* God appreciates Job's excellence.

This God is not like the pagan gods and goddesses, who desire only adoration and obedience. Yes, He promulgates rules. But they are for our good. In the Hebrew and Christian account, God knows the world best because He is the architect. He is the Creator; we are the creatures. And He knows our weaknesses and limitations. So, like a loving parent, He gives us rules to guide us toward the good and away from evil.

When the Hebrew God gives commands to His people, His commands are not arbitrary. Rather, each command serves some good purpose. "See, I have set before you today life and good, death, and evil," Moses told the people of Israel, as he delivered to them the law of God:

> If you obey the commandments of the Lord your God that I command you today, by loving the Lord your God, by walking in His ways, and by keeping His commandments and His statutes and His rules, then you shall live and multiply, and the Lord your God will bless you in the land that you are entering to take possession of it. But if your heart turns away, and you will not hear, but are drawn away to worship other gods and serve them, I declare to you today, that you shall surely perish. (Deuteronomy 30:15–18)

Those options are frequently paired in that way: goodness and life on one side; evil and death on the other. In the Hebrew and Christian account, divine commands are not arbitrary rules promulgated by a prudish God who wants to deprive you of all your fun. On the contrary, the law of God directs us to full life, true enjoyment, genuine flourishing, and it keeps us away from the path of hollow and diminishing pleasures that bear no fruit and lead, ultimately, to death. The point of each commandment is to secure some good that God has given to us.

For example, the good secured by the Sixth Commandment is human life itself, God's greatest and most sacred gift to us and the gift over which he has given us the most limited jurisdiction. Human life is not ours to make by ourselves, and it is not ours to take intentionally. Human life is valuable all by itself; its worth is intrinsic to itself. Human life has value simply because it is human life. And so we can never justify intentional killing. No other good is more important or more valuable than human life. That's why God forbids us to kill deliberately, period. Murder is a moral absolute because human life is an intrinsic good, and therefore, the intentional destruction of innocent human life is intrinsically evil.

The Sixth Commandment's *immediate* concern—the choice between life and death—is the *ultimate* concern of the whole of the Ten Commandments. The Sixth Commandment is about the immediate choice between bodily life and bodily death. The Ten Commandments are about the many choices we make on a daily basis between the life and death of our characters or souls. The two are connected, of course. The choice to commit murder is a dramatic and consequential choice of evil and death. But it is not the only path to evil and death. If we steal or lie and do not repent of those actions, eventually, we strangle our capacity for generosity and truthfulness. The Ten Commandments all are designed to keep us on the path that leads to fullness and life and off the path that leads to the destruction of our good nature.

Opposite to the error of making God out to be inscrutable are those who think that religious people overemphasize the concept of sin and make it out to be more important than it is. Those mentioned here, who value acceptance and tolerance, reject the idea of a God who judges sin. They think that to judge a person's actions is to reject the person. They identify judgment with intolerance, even bigotry.

To many people, this view seems indifferent to wrongdoing and injustice. It can only be held by people who enjoy the benefits of the rule of law and take for granted the redress of wrongs. Almost no one who has ever lived throughout human history, except for affluent Westerners today, has any difficulty understanding that a good God judges sin and wrongdoing. Anyone who has experienced the sins of the world and is not desensitized to them will see clearly that a good God *must* exercise judgment, else He could not possibly be good, and that humans should do the same. That many of us do not understand this reveals just how privileged we are and how insulated we are from the evil that humans routinely perpetrate against each other. And it suggests that we do not understand the extent to which our own choices and actions contribute to a culture of wrongdoing.

Most of human history is full of wrongdoing and injustice. And sin continues to characterize human action throughout the world today. It would be tragic to reject the legalist conception of God only to accept a conception of God as tolerant of injustice. The tolerant God does not seem concerned with evil. In particular, He seems not to be concerned about those who suffer injustice.

Those who suffer from and abhor evil (e.g., bonded servants, sex slaves, war refugees, and the people who labor on their behalf) understand and desire justice. A Nigerian man whose wife and children are murdered by Fulani jihadists has no difficulty making judgments about sin and wrongdoing. Someone whose Sudanese village has been razed by the Janjaweed Militia has no difficulty accepting the idea that we should condemn wrongdoing. To condemn the actions of her oppressors is to begin to vindicate her cause. A girl who is kept as a sex slave for the use of ISIS soldiers hopes and prays that someone is willing to exercise right judgment. The idea of sin would be intelligible to a Uighur child whose parents have been hauled by the Chinese government to a reeducation camp, a North Korean citizen whose government is starving him to death, and a victim of Stalin, Mao, Pol Pot, or any of the other totalitarian thugs of the last 100 years.

Those are extreme examples. They should not lead us to think that we are immune from wrongdoing. We do not understand the extent to which our own choices and actions contribute to wrongdoing and suffering. Not enough of us stop before purchasing a consumer good to consider how our purchase might contribute to the displacement of people or pollution on the other side of the world. We do not often contemplate how our consumption of sexually suggestive and explicit media contributes to the supply and demand for exploitation of girls and young women. We have not sufficiently examined the extent to which prioritizing the desires of adults for intimacy and personal fulfillment has long-term implications for children. We do not understand all the causes of mass shootings and mass incarceration, nor the extent to which we contribute to a culture that disserves young men who desire to be feared if they cannot earn respect.

Around the world and throughout history, humans have understood that no god can claim to be good and loving who is not also just. A loving God must care deeply about the wrongs we do and the suffering we cause to each other. A loving God cannot be indifferent to sin. Like the legalist who posits a narcissistic or arbitrary God, those who posit an indifferent God misunderstand human nature and the human condition. The Hebrew and Christian idea of sin makes the best sense of who we are and what has gone wrong with us.

WHAT SIN IS

If we are going to work together toward what is right, then we would benefit from recovering a more sophisticated and complete understanding of human nature and human action. And a correct conception of sin would help us achieve that understanding. Sin is the irremediable destruction and unmaking of the created order, which is good. Our human nature is the crown of the created order, the most godlike good in the world. In other words, other people are not the ultimate enemy. Sin is our enemy. And any of us can fall prey to this enemy at any time.

To understand this point, we need to go back to the beginning of the religious traditions that gave us the idea of sin. The Apostle John teaches Christians that at the beginning of all time was the word, the Logos. The creative word is the source of order and goodness in the world. Similarly, we read in the Hebrew scriptures that God spoke the world into existence. He uttered the words, "Let there be rainbow trout," and the DNA of rainbow trout sprang into being.

According to these traditions, when God said, "Let us make man in our own image," He created male and female with the inherent logic of male and female human beings. God spoke Adam and Eve into existence, just as He had already spoken the stars and the trees and the rainbow trout into existence. But with Adam and Eve, He did something more. He also fashioned them with His own hand and breathed His spirit and image into them. He made them animals, but He made them *rational* animals, with the power to reason and choose what is good. In the Hebrew account of creation, God told Adam and Eve to exercise dominion over the created order, over all the other created beings who do not have the powers of reason and choice. He delegated to them part of His authority to order the world.

To be created in the image of God is an awesome state of existence. It is the power to create new goods, to bring new good states of affairs into being that are contingent, that would not exist but for our reasoning and choosing and laboring in the world, just as the world would not exist but for His speaking it into existence. Therefore, Adam and Eve and their descendants have built cities and parks and gardens; composed symphonies and operas and ballets; written stories and novels. Michelangelo created the David, Johan Sebastian Bach created the *Mass in B Minor* and the Contrapunctus Fugues, Shakespeare created *Hamlet*, Justinian and his jurists created the *Institutes* and Blackstone wrote his *Commentaries on the Laws of England*, and Thomas Edison created the lightbulb and Alexander Graham Bell the telephone.

And none of these good things were inevitable. All of them were contingent at the moment of creation. For every human being has the power to choose. And so, it could have been otherwise. We might never have had fugues and symphonies and novels and cathedrals and skyscrapers and light bulbs. And we know this because it is otherwise in most of the world throughout most of human history. For the vast majority of people who have ever lived, life is not full of these treasures, but is rather, in the famous words of Thomas Hobbes, nasty, poor, solitary, brutish, and short.

The reason for this, Christians say, is that the radical human power to *choose the good* is also, inherently and unavoidably, the radical power to *choose evil*. That word, "evil," is not spoken very much in polite high society today. Many of our neighbors are in denial about the human condition. They insist on believing that human progress is inevitable and ultimately triumphant, despite the overwhelming evidence to the contrary. Therefore, they do not understand what sin is.

Sin is just the unmaking of good order, either a good order given in nature or a good order created by human beings. Consider: What is it to commit murder? It is to destroy, permanently and for eternity, the life of a human being. It is to bring to a premature end a human life that bears the image of God, a radical cause of good states of affairs, which was to be lived within time and space but never will be lived out because of the act of murder.

Therefore, to murder is not just to kill the body. For a human life is not just a bodily life but also a sequence of moments of radical agency within time, each of which projects infinitely into eternity. What it means to be human, and not merely a physical body or an animal, is to exercise the radical power of rational choice, that great and godlike power, in each present moment and, thus, to shape and even alter the trajectory of eternity for good or ill.

In the Christian account, human life is a sequence of acts of creation and destruction, each radiating out or not throughout history (and maybe beyond) according to the choices and actions made in each moment. An act of murder is, therefore, not just an evil act at the moment in which it occurs but also an evil act in each moment that would have occurred in the victim's life but for the killing and every timeline that would have grown out of each of those moments. To end a life is to destroy this moment and all the good that this divine image-bearer might have brought into eternal being at this moment, and it is to destroy the next moment and the line of good that might have come about in it, and the next, and the next, and so on. To kill a human being is to kill all the possible worlds that human being might have brought into being.

Something analogous occurs, with equally awesome and eternal consequences, when we sin against a good ordered by human beings. Consider the good of friendship. A friendship is one of those good orders that humans have the capacity to bring about by our own choices and actions, that depends not only on given nature but also on our act of creation. To form a friendship, two people must choose to adopt each other's good as their own reason for choices and actions. A friendship is a real and genuine good for both friends because each wants what is best for the other. And each wants the other's good because each chooses to make the other's good his own good as well. It could be otherwise. One can choose to be indifferent toward other people, or even to hate them. We have the power to choose to bring about the friendship or not.

If we choose friendship, then we are both better off. And not only are we better off. The good of friendship radiates out beyond the two people who form it. We all know friendships that produce and spin off rich, complex, and socially expensive goods that benefit many other people, even many hundreds or thousands or millions of people. Consider, for example, the friendship of David and Jonathan, described in the Bible, which saved the nation of Israel from destruction by the Philistines. Or consider the friendship of C. S. Lewis and J. R. R. Tolkien, who encouraged each other to write masterful works such as *The Chronicles of Narnia* and the *Lord of the Rings* trilogy. Their friendship was the source of beautiful works of fiction that have enriched generations of people throughout the English-speaking world.

To destroy a friendship is, therefore, to commit an awesome evil. To defame a friend and steal his reputation, or to lie to him and destroy his trust in you, is not only to act unjustly in that moment, it also is to destroy all of the many moments and all of the many goods that might have come out of those moments of friendship that would have been but for the sinful act. The costs of sin are immeasurable.

WHAT SIN MEANS ABOUT US

The Hebrew tradition of the Ten Commandments encapsulates this two-sided nature of sin. The first five Commandments concern what is given to us, what is good in and of itself, and what we discover to be true whether or not we choose to believe it. The Fifth and Sixth Commandments pivot from what is given toward what is not yet, what is good when chosen well and evil when chosen badly, and what we can make of the world. The second half of the Commandments set before us today and in each moment of our lives life and good, death and evil, and demand that we choose what sort of world we will make of the good world that we have.

The Christian scholar and author C. S. Lewis wrote that "the Present is the point at which time touches eternity. Of the present moment, and of it only, humans have an experience analogous to the experience which [God] has of reality as a whole; in it alone freedom and actuality are offered them." Here Lewis is drawing upon centuries of Christian thought about what it means to be created in the image of God. It means, among other things, that Adam and Eve and their sons and daughters bear God's image by virtue of our radical capacity to speak and to reason and, thus, to order the world to good ends, as God commanded us to do in the garden.

Humans can bring about new good states of affairs, new artifacts and traditions and cultures, and even new human lives. Of course, the same capacity to bring about new goods by our choices and actions is also the capacity to bring about great evils, to destroy and tear down and annihilate. The human power to make the *Brandenburg Concertos* is also the power to make *Mein Kampf*. The human power to make penicillin is also the human power to make the hydrogen bomb.

If we miss this, then we miss the whole point of the second tablet of the Ten Commandments. We should dwell upon our radical, awful, terrifying capacity to bring into being new worlds. We are exercising this capacity at every moment of every day of our lives, whether we think about it or not. We cannot avoid exercising these powers. We can only avoid doing it for good. We are always choosing either the road that leads to goodness and life or the road that leads to evil and death. Best if we consult the road map.

The stakes are also personal. Every choice we make shapes not only the world around us but also *us*. Every time we choose life or death, the pathway that we choose enters into our character and remains there unless and until we repent of it. Someone who lies becomes a liar; someone who steals becomes a thief; someone who commits adultery becomes an adulterer; someone who commits murder becomes a murderer.

None of us is innocent, even if we never commit an act of murder. The disposition at the core of an act of murder is the failure to choose and act toward a human being with respect for that human being's intrinsic worth. It is to treat another human being as not good in and of himself but rather as a mere means to my own ends. Each of us takes this disposition into our character—into our souls—every time we treat another human being as a mere means, and not as an end in himself or herself. This is why Christian tradition has located not just murder in the Sixth Commandment but also suicide, abortion, slavery, usury, and even, in certain cases, defamation or scandal. The great Christian philosopher Thomas Aquinas said that one way to kill another is "by word of mouth." By "provocation, accusation, or detraction," we become culpable in the actions of those who act on our words.

"Thou shalt not kill." That, of course, was the King James translation that served as the cornerstone of jurisprudence throughout the English-speaking world for several centuries. Today, the Anglican prayer book renders it, "Thou shall not murder." There is warrant for both renderings. The Sixth Commandment is given fuller specification in Exodus Chapter 21. There, we read in verse 12, "Whoever strikes a man so that he dies shall be put to death." So far, this is consistent with other ancient codes of the ancient world, such as the Code of Hammurabi, which prescribed punishment for all acts of killing, without regard to the willfulness or malice of the act. The reason was that killing harms the king's good order. An act of killing is wrong because its consequence is to deprive the kingdom of a productive member.

But the God of the Hebrews does not stop there. The passage goes on to specify a defense for nonintentional acts of killing. "But if he did not lie in wait for him, but God let him fall into his hand, then I will appoint for you a place to which he may flee. But if a man willfully attacks another to kill him by cunning, you shall take him from my altar, that he may die." The scripture suggests that willful killing is morally different than acts that cause death but are not intended to kill. Unintentional killing is not culpable in the way that willful killing is.

This is novel and significant. The God of Israel is as interested in the interior aspect of killing—the intention and will of the actor—as He is in the external consequences of the act in the material world. His commands address themselves not only to the political order of His people but also and primarily to their moral and spiritual order. Unlike the pagan gods, the God of Israel is chiefly concerned with what kind of people His people will make of themselves, what moral condition they will form in their own hearts, minds, and habits.

Thus, God's law is both less exacting and more exacting than the other codes of the ancient world. It is less exacting in that innocent killing is not deemed culpable, and the innocent killer is permitted to escape to a sanctuary city. It is more exacting in that someone can violate the Sixth Commandment without actually killing anyone, by willing harm to one's brother or sister and acting in some way on that evil disposition.

In fact, Christian tradition teaches that simply acting in anger against your brother can violate the Sixth Commandment. In his Sermon on the Mount, Christ said:

> You have heard that it was said to those of old, "You shall not murder; and whoever murders will be liable to judgment." But I say to you that everyone who is angry with his brother will be liable to judgment; whoever insults his brother will be liable to the council; and whoever says, "You fool!" will be liable to the hell of fire. (Matthew 5:21–22)

Commenting on this, the medieval Christian philosopher Thomas Aquinas observed that Christ himself got angry, "in whom was the full fountainhead of wisdom," so our Savior cannot mean to condemn *all* acts done in anger. Good judgment and righteous anger are both virtuous. But, Aquinas continues, "There is a third kind of anger which overthrows the judgment of reason and is always sinful, sometimes mortally. . . . " Anger is a mortal sin when we give in to the impulse to avenge an injury we have suffered by returning injury for injury. But none of us has ever done that, right?

The Anglican Catechism asks, "What does it mean not to murder?" It answers:

Since God declares human life sacred from conception to natural death, I may not take the life of neighbors unjustly, bear them malice in my heart, or harm them by word or deed; rather, I should seek to cause their lives to flourish. (Genesis 9:6; Leviticus 19:16; Deuteronomy 19:4–7)

Each of us shares some measure of the culpability of Cain, whose brother's very blood cries out from the ground to God for vindication. None of us is entirely innocent of the Sixth Commandment. Our culpability is only a matter of degree. This should cause us to hesitate before condemning others as irremediably evil, even the very worst among us. Perhaps the person standing in front of you is evil. But their condition is not alien to you. If the Hebrew and Christian account gets anything right about our condition, it is that none of us has complete immunity to sin. We would do well to remember this when criticizing the failures of others.

NOTE

1. https://avalon.law.yale.edu/19th_century/lincoln2.asp.

NINE

The Power of Indifference

DESTRUCTIVE AND CONSTRUCTIVE INDIFFERENCE

Love and hate are powerful dispositions. And they attract a lot of attention. Slogans such as "love wins" and "resist hate" reflect our awareness of the power of love and hate to shape human identity and interactions. We are preoccupied—almost obsessed—with the longing of the human heart to be loved and the profound fear that someone will hate who we are. The yearning to be accepted and the dread of being rejected motivates us to seek relationships with people in whom we might not otherwise have any interest and to avoid people—even our own family—who do not accept us for who we are.

The lavish attention we pay to love and hate often causes us to overlook a third disposition that is equally as powerful. Indeed, it influences our interactions with each other even more powerfully than love and hate precisely because we do not notice its influence. It sneaks up on us and quietly directs our conversations and interactions without revealing its identity. This powerful disposition is indifference.

Indifference can be either constructive or destructive. Like nitroglycerin, it can either heal or demolish. The indifference of a tyrant or an oppressive government is the best hope for some people, especially powerless minorities. Meanwhile, the indifference of a parent, teacher, role model, or other people in a close relationship of care or custody can utterly destroy one's hopes. Therefore, by thinking about indifference, we can learn a lot about how to get along with each other reasonably and about what not to do.

A father who is indifferent to the health of his daughter, a friend who is indifferent to her friend's achievements, a teacher who is indifferent to the education of his students—these people fail to give something valuable that is in their power to give, which they have some reason or even obligation to give. In this way, they impoverish someone. And the person who suffers the indifference experiences the impoverishment as a loss, even if they do not feel it right away.

Consider a father who withholds approval from his son. The son desires and seeks his father's approval. He follows his father's every suggestion. The son enjoys running races and is good at it, but the father makes it known that he prefers baseball to track and field. Therefore, the boy strives to excel at baseball. However, his ambition is futile because the father will not play with him. The boy plays baseball whenever he can with other boys in the neighborhood. When no one is available, he throws tennis balls against the wall of the toolshed for hours at a time. He frequently asks his father to play catch with him, but the father is always too busy.

Despite his incessant efforts, the boy never improves very much. His father's indifference causes the son to lack confidence in his abilities. And when tryouts come for baseball teams, he plays down to the level at which he expects himself to perform. His baseball career peters out in disappointment.

The boy carries this failure with him for the rest of his life.

The father's indifference to the boy's interests and desire to please and impress his father shaped the boy for the worse. It deformed the boy's self-understanding. It leaves a void that the boy feels often, and it is a burden of which the boy cannot rid himself. The burden weighs him down wherever he goes and whatever he tries to do.

Indifference is powerful. Moreover, to be indifferent to someone is sometimes an unjust wrong and profound injury. On the other hand, it can also be a welcome relief from wrong and injury. Indifference can liberate. Imagine a different father, who has strong opinions about every aspect of his son's life. The father's opinions are arbitrary, even unpredictable. He expresses his disapproval of his son's clothes (which are modest and culturally appropriate), friends (who are respectful and responsible), music (which is neither high art nor vulgar or obscene), favorite sports teams, manner of speech, hobbies, and much else.

If one day the father suddenly stopped expressing his opinions, then the son would experience his father's silence as a reprieve. The father still does not approve of his son's choices and actions, but he tolerates them. And tolerance is a good bit better than constant haranguing.

Therefore, indifference is powerful. And like many powers, it can be employed for good or evil. We can generalize from these relatively simple examples. By learning about indifference more generally, we might map a way toward tolerance, even when we cannot find our way to approval or agreement. But we might do even more. We might learn how to employ indifference as a powerful force for good.

THE INDIFFERENCE THAT LEADS TO DESPOTISM

Alexis de Tocqueville produced arguably the most trenchant observations of American culture and politics. The nineteenth-century French aristocrat traveled widely throughout the young United States, noting the habits, customs, and ideals that made Americans distinctly American. He wanted to understand the democratic culture of the American people, which made them prosper and motivated them to resist tyranny. The fruit of his efforts, the book known as *Democracy in America*, yielded a vivid picture of nineteenth-century American life in its light and dark aspects. And because Tocqueville was also a student of history and philosophy and much else, he also supplied keen insights into the causes of the great good and the great evils that Americans accomplished.

Tocqueville was particularly fascinated by the American ideals of liberty and equality. He perceived that these ideals are in tension with each other. While liberty often yields inequality, equality has the potential to destroy liberty. Tocqueville did not think it necessary to choose one over the other. But each had to be tempered by concern for the well-being of one's neighbors. To exercise liberty without regard for the effects of one's actions on others, to ignore the poor and oppressed, is to act unjustly. And to insist on strict equality of result without regard to the needs and merits of others also is to act unjustly. Moreover, these injustices open the door to tyranny.

In Tocqueville's day, Americans took care of each other. That is how they kept tyranny at a distance. And where they acted without regard for others, as in the case of chattel slavery, they allowed tyranny to dwell among them and to destroy their ideals and their trust in each other. Liberty does not by itself cause oppression. But selfish liberty—licentiousness—does.

Equality also can tend to tyranny, not by itself, but when it is focused on the self. If it is not shaped by moral concern for the well-being of others, equality devolves into envy and indifference. Those vices erode ordered liberty and open the door to despotism. Tocqueville remarked the following:

> No vice of the human heart is so acceptable to [despotism] as selfishness: a despot easily forgives his subjects for not loving him, provided they do not love one another. He does not ask them to assist him in governing the state; it is enough that they do not aspire to govern it themselves. . . . Thus the vices which despotism produces are precisely those which equality fosters. These two things perniciously complete and assist each other. Equality places men side by side, unconnected by any common tie; despotism raises barriers to keep them asunder; the former predisposes them not to consider their fellow creatures, the latter makes general indifference a sort of public virtue.

Tocqueville understood that indifference to others is the condition that enables tyranny to grow. When we stop caring for each other and focus only on our own needs and desires, then each of us stops looking to other people for comfort and society. Tyrants step in to meet the human needs that we used to meet for each other. This increases the tyrant's power and weakens rival powers. He, therefore, wants us to be indifferent toward each other.

Preventing tyranny is not the only reason to consider other people's well-being and act on their behalf. To meet the needs of another person is to make that other person better off. It is also to make one's self better off. Those are both reasons in themselves not to be indifferent to others. By feeding a hungry person, I improve his material condition, his physical health. His health is good just because it is the health of a human being. It does not matter whether or not he contributes any wealth or income to the gross domestic product. It matters not whether he creates anything worthwhile or forms any new friendships or authors any new insights or knowledge. That he is healthy and well-fed is a better state of affairs than if he were sickly and hungry. And that's enough.

Furthermore, a person who does something good for someone else improves herself. She makes herself—constitutes herself—as a doer-of-good. Just as someone who lies tends to become a liar and someone who kills becomes a murderer, a person who says true and gracious things about others becomes an encourager, and a person who saves another's life becomes a life-saver. Our choices and actions make us who we are, for better or worse.

Thus, the greatest danger of being indifferent is that we will cause ourselves to become indifferent. If we look for opportunities to help those in need, then we might find them, and we might get better at finding them. By contrast, if we choose to ignore the plight of those who suffer from need or injustice, then, eventually, we will train ourselves how to ignore it, and we might become really good at ignoring it. We might teach ourselves not to see and hear cries for right and justice. We might grow desensitized to injustice and incapable of desiring what is right and just.

THE INDIFFERENCE THAT LEADS TO ORDERED LIBERTY

Indifference to the well-being of others is a powerful corrosive force on the social bonds that hold us together. Nor should we be indifferent to injustice and wrongdoing. It causes injury to the victim and harms the moral character of the wrongdoer. But at the same time, we could all use a bit more indifference concerning our moral differences. Part of what ails our discourse is that we want everyone to share the same moral vision and sense of social justice. And some people either cannot or will not tolerate legitimate moral differences. Not everyone must pursue the same goods by the same means. On matters that properly are indifferent, on which reasonable minds might disagree or which might vary according to context, more toleration of our differences could go a long way.

As we saw in Chapters 6 and 7, natural law teaches us certain moral boundaries. It contains a (very) few moral absolutes, exceptionless duties not to kill, maim, rape, enslave, and defame. Moreover, it teaches us several categorical duties not to take other's things and ideas without permission, not to break our promises, and not to violate another's bodily integrity. Though not absolute, the duties we must exclude ourselves from are things that do not belong to us, fulfill our promises, and avoid physical contact without consent, are robust. Only in certain circumstances, and only for limited categories of reasons, can we justify entering someone's home, breaking a promise, or touching without the interested person's consent.

However, as we also saw in Chapters 6 and 7, most of the practical questions we face on a daily basis are not settled by absolute or categorical duties. Most of our practical reasoning concerns not what we must not do but rather what we should do. And what we should do differs from person to person, context to context. It is contingent upon our prior commitments and obligations, the resources available to us, the merits of the person who is making a claim for our action or benefaction, and much else.

Legal and philosophical thinkers have long referred to this sort of question as matters of indifference. This does not mean that we should not care about what is to be done. On the contrary, it means that settling what is to be done is partly our responsibility. As Aristotle explained more than two thousand years ago, a matter of indifference is one that can be conclusively settled and determined in various, reasonable ways. There is not one, uniquely correct answer. Reasonable minds might disagree. The answer might be contingent upon circumstances and other obligations. The answer might even change over time as circumstances change.

In other words, in matters of indifference, people have at least some freedom to choose what to do. In some cases, people have perfect freedom to choose. The matter is not determined by what reason requires. There is no one truth. Rather, it is the choice itself that determines the right answer for that person or group, in that time and place, in light of the particular circumstances.

Consider again the example of parents raising their children. The parents have an obligation to raise their children to be as healthy, knowledgeable, and self-sufficient as possible, given the resources and opportunities available to them. But the obligation is open-ended. It can reasonably be satisfied in different ways according to circumstances.

Also, and as importantly, it can reasonably be determined in a different way according to the choices the parents make. Given the same resources and opportunities and given similar children with the same interests and abilities, different parents can reasonably choose to raise their children differently. For example, some parents might read to their children books that emphasize practical and vocational skills while others might spend time teaching their children the great books of human history. Still others might choose literature drawn from a particular ethnic culture, or from a variety of cultures.

PRIVATE AND PLURAL ORDERS

The choices parents make constitute the family in particular ways and not in others. A family that travels the world together is a different kind of family than one that spends its vacations at the beach. In constituting a family identity, the opportunities and options that the parents do *not* choose are at least as important as those they *do* choose. Imagine parents who choose to be agrarian, to make a living by the sweat of their own brow and to impart to their children self-sufficiency, a love of a particular place, and an appreciation of the land. It will probably be necessary for them to live in a rural community rather than a big city.

Other families might choose instead to live in the city. And that is OK too. Not every family must be the same. The ordering of family life can and should be plural, not unitary (i.e., within the bounds of the moral absolutes, such as norms against child abuse). If every family were the same, not only would the world be a very dull place, but also most families, and most people within families, would not have the opportunities they need to pursue their own good ends.

This lesson can be scaled up from the family to the other groups and associations within society. Different groups within society are formed around different good ends. Universities and colleges are oriented toward the good of knowledge. That is a different end than the good of the family farm, which is to provide food for health and to occupy the family members in a common pursuit and life plan. The good of the trade guild is not that of the symphony orchestra, which is not the same as the football club, which is not the good of the charitable trust, and so forth.

A political society and its agent, which is the state, must be indifferent as between these different groups and associations. It must be indifferent in justice, for the state has no reason to privilege any one of these goods over any others. Knowledge is a different good than friendship. Thus, the good of the university and the good of the fraternal association cannot rationally be compared on a single scale. It cannot be rational to sacrifice the good of the university for the sake of the social club, nor to sacrifice the social club for the sake of the university. When states get in the business of choosing winners and losers in society, they do so arbitrarily and unjustly.

PRIVATE ORDERS AND PRIVATE LAW

To be sure, there must be boundaries around these plural domains and orders. We need some public law. Sometimes we need officials with power to order us to act on a unitary plan. For example, when a society is attacked or threatened by an enemy bent on the society's destruction, it is reasonable for the people to defend themselves. And a people cannot fight a successful war if every member of the society is free to do whatever he or she pleases. And we need criminal laws to restrain perpetrators of serious, public wrongs. And we need law to govern the lawgivers. The moment we have a government strong enough to secure the rule of law and protect the vulnerable, the government becomes capable of destroying the rule of law and exploiting the vulnerable. Therefore, we need constitutions.

Nevertheless, not all law must be the same for everyone. Indeed, most law can be *and should be* plural and private. Many rights and duties cannot reasonably be specified except within particular contexts and upon particular judgments of reasonableness. And the people who decide what is to be done should be the people closest to the situation, with the best knowledge of the context, the most wisdom about the problem, and the most at stake in the solution.

Institutions and norms of private law fill the need of these people to make their own rights and duties to govern their actions. The doctrines and formal requirements of private law supply the needs of the groups and associations of civil society for answers to the Practical Question. The laws of contract and property signal to the family, the university, and the small business which promises will be enforced in court and which uses they may make of their resources without being held liable to their neighbors. This enables these groups to order their actions toward their common goods. And those groups and associations return the favor by specifying private law as particular rights and duties pertaining between persons. Those acts of private lawmaking become data for future legal decision-making.

Every time someone drops off a suit at their local dry-cleaning business, the customer and the dry cleaner are creating their own, private rights and duties. (The thing they create is known in law as a "bailment.") Neighborhood and condominium associations create their own bylaws and rules of conduct. Property owners devise and bequeath their homes and family heirlooms to deserving recipients in their wills and create trusts for the benefit of the very young and to give charitably to deserving causes. A thousand times each day, potential customers walk into open businesses, exercising a legal right conferred upon them by the business owner called a "license."

Bailments, bylaws, wills, trusts, and licenses are all laws. They do not come from governments. They come from people who are reasonably ordering their little corners of the world to good ends. They differ from place to place, group to group, and even between different transactions within the same community because the people are making them.

Most people do not stop to reflect upon the remarkable power they exercise each day to make their own law and generate their own obligations as they purchase event tickets, sign rental-car agreements, and purchase insurance policies. Indeed, some people are unaware that they are promulgating their own law. But, in fact, each of us is a lawmaker. And this fact is morally significant.

Making private law is an important way in which we author our own lives, both as individuals and in groups and associations. As groups of persons settle and specify their rights and duties, they constitute themselves and their members as groups and associations of particular kinds. The university is constituted by different rights and duties than the family, whose norms differ quite radically from the trade union and the stock exchange.

Groups, like individuals, engage in morally significant acts of self-constitution. Indeed, for voluntary associations (as compared to natural communities, such as the family), the act of making the group's private law gives associations their existence. Without a charter, bylaws, and mission statement, a corporation or nonprofit charitable organization would quite literally not exist as a legal person.

Such communities as voluntary associations exist as realities because they choose particular laws to govern their own choices and actions instead of others. They make their own plans of action to achieve shared goals, and they make their own rules and obligations to carry out the plans. Without shared ends, an agreed-upon plan of action for achieving those ends and assigned responsibilities and obligations to carry out the plan, there would be no association or voluntary community, only a collection of individuals who may or may not happen to be doing the same thing. The very fact that humans can coordinate their actions in this way raises the possibility of communal self-constitution, which is richer than the individual self-authorship discussed in Chapter 6.

THE IMPORTANCE OF DISCRIMINATION

Private law norms, such as property and contract rights, enable groups to adopt those norms that advance the group's common good and that shape the actions and characters of the group's members for that good. For example, private property ownership enables groups and societies of people to refuse to sanction actions that are inconsistent with their plans of action and, therefore, with their identity. One becomes a person or group that acts in pursuit of reason x in part by not acting for not-x and, in part, by not acting for reasons y and z. Without the authority to exclude those who would involve the group in acting for reasons not-x, y, and z, the owners and their collaborators could not define their commitments, and therefore, they could not constitute themselves around those commitments.

In other words, people must be free to discriminate. "Discrimination" has become an unpopular word today because political communities such as South Africa during Apartheid and states in the American South during Jim Crow segregation authorized, and even required, discrimination on the basis of race. Racial discrimination is inherently unjust. It violates the equal and inherent dignity of persons. But that some forms of discrimination are evil and unjust does not mean that all discrimination is evil and unjust. To the contrary, some discrimination is entailed in, or even required by, natural law.

Discrimination is simply another word for making distinctions. Because distinctions can be either good or evil, discrimination can be either just or unjust. To distinguish between white people and black people in deciding whom to serve or do business with is to distinguish contrary to reason. Race is morally arbitrary. And to employ race as the criterion for choice and action is to deprive a class of persons of the equal status that through justice they should enjoy. Race is a bad basis for distinctions between people, and therefore, racial discrimination is unjust.

However, other criteria are not arbitrary or evil. Indeed, some are essential. Imagine answering a loud knock on your door in the middle of the night. Just outside the door you see a nun, frantic and terrified. Behind the nun, approaching quickly in a menacing posture, is a large man wearing a hockey mask and wielding a hatchet. It is reasonable to discriminate in favor of the nun and against the mask-wearing psycho. Let her in; keep him out.

Less fancifully, we all make rational distinctions on a daily basis. And often, we discriminate for the purpose of preserving the communities of which we are part. I might feed someone else's children, but my primary obligation is to feed my own. If I have only enough food for my own, then it is not irrational to feed my own first. My natural duties to, and affection for, my own children are valid reasons to do what I can to help them flourish even if I cannot make everyone's children flourish.

The same principle applies to larger communities. A community that is committed to nonviolence, such as the Amish, constitutes itself as that kind of community by exercising its right to exclude weapons manufacturers. Indeed, the Amish could not be Amish were they not at liberty to discriminate against those who make weapons.

Thus, the liberties and powers of communities to form their own domains are necessary to realize all the goods of a human society. Private rights perform not just economic work but also moral work. The ability of a group to answer the Practical Question in its own way and to form its own rights and duties accordingly—to form its own moral commitments—is an essential component of a well-ordered and flourishing society. And it is essential not only for individual people but also for groups and communities of individuals who work together for a common good.

The College Democrats could not maintain the integrity of their mission were they not allowed to promulgate their own bylaws requiring all of their officers to profess adherence to the platform of the Democratic Party. Civil rights organizers of bus boycotts and sit-ins in the 1950s and 1960s could not have made and executed their plans had they not had the right to exclude segregationists from their meetings on private property. A religious community cannot preserve its moral teachings if it cannot refuse to ordain clergy who deny those teachings.

This is why our law contains a presumption in favor of liberty. And it is why our tradition is full of private law. Governments should not deprive people of opportunities and powers to govern themselves because self-governance is an essential aspect of self-authorship.

Sometimes it is necessary for the political community to promulgate public laws in order to achieve particular goods by discrete plans of action. For example, to protect streams and rivers from pollutants, it might not always be enough to have private property. If the water is a common resource or owned by a large number of owners, then the people who use the water might not have sufficient incentives to conserve and protect the water from harm. Therefore, we might need criminal and administrative laws prohibiting harm to our water. Similarly, we might need a scheme of general laws, applicable to everyone in the same way, if we want to ensure the timely and safe delivery of the mail, a system of taxation that treats everyone fairly, and a way to secure commerce across state lines.

However, unless it is necessary to regulate some action by public law, legislators and public officials should refrain from making public laws to govern actions that are currently governed by private laws. The plurality of the common good requires robust protection for private rights and duties. Justice in and for our social interactions—social justice—requires us to secure property and contract, the liberty of the family and the family business and the Amish. We must enable different groups the freedom to constitute themselves differently. Though we do not owe groups freedom to do what must not be done, such as enslaving or defaming, in most other respects, we can and should tolerate their different answers to the Practical Question.

That is a source of hope in our fractured and fractious age. Most of the moral truth that ought to direct our practical reasoning is indeterminate.

It consists of matters of indifference that can reasonably be specified in various ways. Therefore, private law is and ought to be pluralist. It enables the groups and associations of civil society to pursue plural and incommensurable goods. Those groups pursue their various common goods within the bounds of their absolute duties by making their own concrete rights and duties.

DIFFERENT GOODS FOR DIFFERENT GROUPS

If we want to reason well together and to see each other flourish, then we need the right kind of indifference. We should not be indifferent to inherent wrongs or to injustice. However, we should hesitate before trying to answer the Practical Question for a group or association of people of which we are not part, in whose shared good we do not participate, and whose reasons we do not understand.

That is perhaps a bit abstract. What does good indifference look like in practice? In practice, people build their associations and institutions differently according to the different goods each group pursues. A soup kitchen has different rules and expectations than a college because each is designed to bring about different aspects of human well-being. A group of people organized for the purpose of feeding the hungry certainly are concerned about the overall health and well-being of the people whom they serve, but their primary objective is to make sure that people who come to their kitchen receive nutrition and calories. If the soup kitchen servers do not teach anyone any useful knowledge, they have not failed in their mission. However, if people go away hungry, that is a failure. The college might well provide food services for its students, but that service is secondary to the college's mission, which is imparting knowledge of truth to the students. When students leave for the summer, the college does not continue to feed them. But the students should leave with more knowledge than they possessed when they came.

The right thing to do in each case is determined largely by the good ends that each institution is attempting to bring about. Therefore, the soup kitchen will follow conventions—whether explicit rules or simply coordinated actions—that ensure the efficient delivery of nutritious food to as many people as possible. The college dining services, by contrast, might work toward not volume but variety. The soup kitchen will enlist volunteers. The college will pay its staff. The soup kitchen will charge those whom it serves only a nominal amount, if anything. The college will charge students at least a market rate. The soup kitchen might serve all comers, while the college will serve only students.

Two institutions that are oriented toward the same good can reasonably differ in how they pursue it. The good of knowledge supplies the practical reasons for a college or university. But different colleges and universities are oriented toward different aspects of knowledge. The engineering college attempts to impart practical knowledge to its students, while the liberal arts college imparts more theoretical understanding. The engineering college imparts knowledge of science and the useful arts because that knowledge is instrumentally valuable for solving problems in the world. The liberal arts college imparts knowledge because knowledge is good to have for its own sake; students are better off who have asked important questions and have sought good answers. This difference, too, will result in different practices.

Even two institutions that are oriented toward the same aspect of the same good might turn out differently. After all, people are different. They value different things. They learn differently. They have different strengths and weaknesses. In the last chapter, we will consider a comparison of two groups that are similar but also different enough to warrant different rules, rights, and duties for their members.

TEN

Doing Difference Well

LOWERING THE STAKES, ENABLING PLURALISM

Our civic discourse is so rancorous in part because too much is at stake. If every important question is a zero-sum contest between competing proposals, then someone's proposal must always lose, and the losers must then be governed by proposals that they find to be not merely objectionable but unreasonable or even wrong. But that's "if." What if most of our controversies need not be zero-sum contests? What if we can live out our differences well and reasonably?

We have seen that most controversies about the right thing to do concern particular and contingent concerns rather than universal and absolute rights. People certainly have absolute rights, and they are important. We all have exception-less duties not to enslave and defame, to take two examples, and so we all have absolute rights not to be enslaved or defamed. However, as long as we stay within the moral boundaries marked off by those important duties of *abstention*, we have great freedom to settle on particular duties of *action* and the rights that correlate with them. Parents and teachers have obligations to educate and care for children. But not everyone must educate their children or students the same way or feed them the same food.

We have also seen that most important questions in our day are not simple questions that lead to universally true answers. Most are matters of indifference, about which reasonable minds can disagree, or which are contingent on variable circumstances. We can generalize this lesson to legal and policy issues. Different states might adopt different tax policies, for example. One might use an income tax, while another may rely more heavily on property and sales taxes. And which tax a state employs might depend in part on conditions within that state. A state with a primarily agricultural-based economy might find it prudent to use a different combination of taxes than a state with an industrial economy, or one built on information technologies.

In short, we can have pluralism. We can and should encourage different groups and communities of people to explore a variety of different answers to our practical questions and different solutions to our problems, as long as they do not infringe absolute, fundamental rights or commit inherent wrongs. Allowing a greater variety of options and more freedom to choose between them would return practical reasoning to the domain of the practical. It would avoid many of our zero-sum contests, would lower the stakes in our disagreements, and would likely lower the temperature of our discourse.

This is one reason why central planning and centralized governments are unwise. The more responsibility that we cede to central governments over our lives, and the more important practical questions that we commit to public law, the less room there is for civil and reasonable disagreement. Governments operate on general rules that apply the same to everyone. They can only allow one right answer, even when other answers would be equally reasonable or more so.

The alternative to centralized government is private property. In our legal tradition, the diversity of human goods within society is made possible by private property rights. This is a reason why the due process clauses of the Fifth and Fourteenth Amendments to the Constitution of the United States list property along with life and liberty as one of the most fundamental and important rights. The point of property rights is to enable and secure the freedom of different groups to pursue different goods within society. We need not all value the same things. We can have differences. No one size must fit all.

Classically, these plural orders are known as the "domains" of society. Different individuals, groups, and associations can operate differently within their various domains because their property rights free them to decide for themselves what to do. We do not always, or even often, need to play the same game by the same rules according to the same plan of action.

The various domains of society are protected within the domains of private property rights. The domain of parents is the home, where they can raise their children according to their own convictions. Their right to decide who enters their home and their right to use their home as they see fit enable them to make their own plans for the life of their family. Different parents raise their children differently. And that is OK.

Private property rights do the same work in public that they do in private homes. Different business owners have different values. Property rights free and empower them to operate their businesses according to their values, and employees are free to choose employers whose values they share. A religious employee can choose to work in a religious company (e.g., one that keeps the Sabbath and refuses to subsidize birth control, perhaps) while a nonreligious employee can choose to work for a company that has more immanent values (e.g., one that stays open all week and subsidizes birth control as part of its benefits package).

Different groups of people can answer the Practical Question differently if they have the liberty and powers necessary to answer the Practical Question for themselves. This is true not only for families and businesses but also for religious associations, charitable organizations, schools and colleges and universities, sporting and social clubs, and all the other groups and associations within society where people find provision and meaning.

DOMAINS OF KNOWLEDGE

To see how this works in education, consider two different hypothetical colleges. Let us call them "Authenticity College" and "Virtue College." Both are fictitious, and their features are exaggerated for purposes of comparison. Like the Four Moralists discussed in Chapter 2, these institutions are caricatures. However, you might recognize some features of actual colleges in their descriptions.

Both Authenticity College and Virtue College are oriented toward the good of knowledge. Both are interested in knowledge for its own sake. They hold themselves out as institutions of learning, and they expect their faculty and students to pursue knowledge together in community. However, the two colleges have different understandings of what knowledge is and different visions for how to acquire it. Each pursues knowledge within its domain—it exercises the powers and liberties of property ownership over its campus and its other resources for the common good of attaining knowledge—but each does so in its own unique way.

Authenticity College's mission and vision statement teach that the most important knowledge to acquire is knowledge of oneself. This college's motto is "To thine own self be true," which reflects its commitment to personal authenticity above all else. The faculty and administration do their best not to privilege any kind of knowledge over any other. The college has no core requirements. It also has no standard format for courses. Both the professors and the students develop courses for students together, either personalized for a single student or for a group of students who are interested in the same subject matter. Courses may be structured as lecture series, seminars, research projects, reading groups, or simply extended conversations.

At Authenticity College, professors do not challenge students' assumptions and convictions. On the contrary, the faculty affirms the beliefs of each student. Students decide when a course of study is completed and perform their own evaluations. They pick the grade that they think best reflects their efforts and achievements. After eight periods of self-assessment, reflecting eight semesters of study, students graduate (usually with honors).

Authenticity College has no code of conduct, honor code, or code of any other kind. Students are expected not to break the law. Students who are convicted of serious crimes while attending the college are often suspended until they have served their sentences, but the college does not otherwise take disciplinary action against students. Students govern themselves by convention. When a student does some act that endangers or calls into question another student's authenticity or personal autonomy, other students generally gather to condemn the action. In serious cases, as where a student accuses another of sexual assault or personal disparagement, the student body will take a vote whether to shun the offending student. If a majority of students vote "yay," then the shunned student is not welcome to attend social events and must sit alone in the library and dining halls. Classmates are discouraged from associating with the shunned student and are shamed publicly if they do.

Virtue College is a different sort of institution. It is organized around a tighter concept of knowledge. The faculty considers knowledge a form of excellence and is interested in knowledge of truth. The college's motto, "Veritas," reflects its orientation toward a better understanding of what the case is objectively. The faculty is not generally interested in the opinions of students except insofar as those opinions come over time to conform more closely to what is excellent and true. The college has a very rigorous core curriculum, which comprises half of the courses required to graduate. It includes the study of time-tested works in the liberal arts, such as ancient Greek and medieval Christian philosophy; Shakespeare's plays and Dante's allegories; Hebrew, Christian, and Muslim scriptures; and the jurisprudence of Justinian, John Locke, and John Adams. It also includes elementary art and music history, physics and chemistry, and history and economics.

At Virtue College, professors challenge students to find the correct answers to difficult questions. Students are evaluated regularly and graded on a curve. Competition is fierce, yet the students quickly identify with each other as co-combatants against their professors, who seem to always be trying to do them in. As a result, the students form lasting bonds and a common identity around having together achieved something difficult and worthwhile.

Virtue College has a precise disciplinary code. All students sign a pledge when they first enroll that they will not violate any provision of the code. The code forbids: lying, gossiping, and slandering any person; cheating and helping others to cheat; getting drunk and brawling. It requires students to: help classmates who struggle academically; obey a curfew and quiet-hour restrictions; and report to the administration any violation of the code that a student witnesses. Administrators take violations seriously. If, after a hearing, the evidence shows that a student violated any provision of the code, then the student is suspended for one semester. If a student commits a second infraction or is charged with any crime, no matter the seriousness of the criminal offense, then the student is expelled.

Obviously, these are idealized types constructed out of core, essential characteristics. Some colleges are more similar to Authenticity College, and others are more similar to Virtue College, though it is unlikely that very many colleges possess all the characteristics of either of them. The point is that how exactly to constitute a college is largely a matter of indifference. Both of these institutions are recognizable as colleges. You might find one model more attractive than the other. You might even form the judgment that one model is better. But to insist that no college should constitute itself as Authenticity College does would be unjust to those who wish to pursue the goods of self-knowledge and authenticity. Similarly, to prohibit colleges such as Virtue College would be unjust to those who desire knowledge of truth and virtue.

Each college can be free to pursue its distinct conception of the good of knowledge if its members can together form their own rules and customs to govern the activities that occur within its domain. And—crucially!—each must be free to reject certain rules, customs, and practices as contrary to its identity. Each must, in short, be free to discriminate between what is right for its own enterprise and what is not.

Authenticity College is committed to helping students express their genuine identity. Virtue College is committed to imparting to students a particular conception of what is good, true, and right. To achieve their different ends, the colleges must be free to impose different rules on their constituent members than other colleges choose for their members. Authenticity College could not pursue the good of personal authenticity as vigorously if faculty and fellow students were permitted to question essential aspects of students' identities. Virtue College could not pursue the good of truth with as much commitment if faculty were to affirm whatever views students happen to hold.

It seems likely that these colleges will produce different graduates. But it seems equally likely that the differences will be tolerable, perhaps even beneficial to society. Knowledge is capacious and has many aspects. Students preparing for different life plans might reasonably learn different aspects of knowledge. Moreover, they might reasonably strive for different virtues. The virtues and knowledge that are characteristic of an excellent soldier or sailor differ from the virtues and knowledge that are characteristic of an excellent artist. Thus, we should not be surprised to find that the program of education at a military academy differs markedly from that of a music conservatory. Therefore, we should operate with a presumption of liberty in education as in other domains of society. We have different colleges and universities because we have plural educational pursuits for a plurality of practical questions.

PLURAL DOMAINS

So, what we seek is a plurality of domains. A diversity of lawful domains makes possible the diversity of educational offerings that we enjoy in the United States. Because we allow different educational institutions to govern themselves, we are not limited to one vision or plan for higher education. We do difference well precisely to the extent that we avoid zero-sum thinking and resist one-size-fits-all answers to the Practical Question.

Our legal and political traditions have a word for this pluralist concept of governance. That word is "dominion," the word that jurists have used to describe private property ownership. It is both the legal means by which people order their actions in a free society and an ideal way of being and acting in the world and bringing about the common good. The word dominion and the idea that it represents comes from an amalgam of Roman law, the Bible, ancient custom, and natural law philosophy. It is foundational to nearly all the free governments that have emerged on the face of the Earth. However, today, it is not well understood.

Dominion enables pluralism because it enables people to live their lives according to their own plans rather than always receiving direction from a single sovereign. Insofar as people act freely and responsibly within their domains—in their homes, on their campuses, in their businesses and charitable organizations—they order part of the world reasonably to good ends that others might not share or even understand. Consider that in the American South in the twentieth century, the Civil Rights movement was birthed in homes and churches, behind the security that private property rights afford. If people have dominion, then they can challenge prevailing orthodoxies, or simply go their own way.

This requires both freedom—liberties to act and powers to make one's own obligations—and responsibility—duties not to wrong others and liability for wrongs done. People can expect governments to refrain from interfering in their domains only to the extent that they do not abuse their freedom to do wrong. A parent who uses his dominion to abuse his children can reasonably expect the state to enter his home and intervene on their behalf. A college that allows its students to assault each other with impunity can reasonably expect the police to enter campus and perform the work that college administrators refuse to perform. Freedom makes pluralism possible only when it is exercised well, or at least when it is not exercised for evil.

So, we need freedom, but freedom must be exercised consistent with our absolute duties. Private property meets this challenge. Property rights secure the liberty and power of owners and their collaborators within various domains to pursue their own goods by plans of their own making. One family can use their property to grow crops, another can use theirs to perform jazz music or musical theater productions. The faculty, staff, and students of Authenticity College organize the life of their campus around one concept of knowledge, Virtue College bases theirs around a different concept. Yet all of these property owners are bound by law. They must all exercise the liberties and powers of ownership so as not to injure the rights of the others. Moreover, they must not use their property to commit intrinsic wrongs.

In our legal tradition, each domain is constituted and marked out by its boundaries, and its boundaries are constituted by the rights of other dominion holders. The rights of one domain are the duties of the next one. Because the farming family has a duty not to pollute the water supply, the musical family next door has a right not to suffer pollution in their water. Because the musical family has a duty not to interfere with the farming family's use of their land, the farming family has a right not to be awakened in the middle of the night by loud music.

DOMINION AS FREEDOM AND RESPONSIBILITY

Plural dominion is not only a way to resolve conflicts. It is also an ideal for life together in a political community. Dominion, in its focal or best sense, is the creative and ordered governance of the natural world by human beings. And because human beings are different, excellent ordering of the world by different human beings in their respective domains has the potential to bring into being a great diversity of human goods. A plurality of domains empowers human beings to be fully human, which is to say, fully awe-inspiring.

Dominion is neither domination nor license, neither tyranny nor anarchy. It is the power and freedom that human beings can exercise to rule their own passions and desires according to what is true and good and then to order their communities also according to the law of reason, the natural law. Dominion enables us to answer the Practical Question for ourselves and to instantiate our particular aspects of the common good. Dominion proceeds first to produce self-governance, then to secure the rule of law for the political community, and then extends to a flourishing civil society, a pluralistic realm in which private and public orders grow together and support each other, all for the benefit of the persons who comprise the society.

The Hebrew and Christian scriptures provide a backstory to the classical idea of dominion. In this account, God spoke his word into the void, and as a result, all that was given as good came into being and all that is potentially good became possible. God sequentially created and ordered the world by the action of his word. He spoke the word "light," and there was light. He spoke the sun and moon and Earth into existence, as well as the dry land and seas. He spoke the word for rainbow trout, and there were rainbow trout.

After creating this world and declaring it very good, God conveyed control over the Earth, the jewel of His creative efforts, to two of His creatures, Adam and Eve. God called their possessory estate "dominion." This dominion is to be "over" all the birds and animals and living things. Adam and Eve and their sons and daughter were meant to take responsibility for the world, to care for it, and to improve it by their creative efforts.

Notice that the dividing line between those who have the delegated power of dominion and those who are subject to it runs between the man and woman, on one side, and the rest of the world on the other. In the Jewish and Christian stories, humans exercise dominion and are responsible for all nonhuman creation. This means that all people who share the nature of Adam and Eve—all human beings—are delegated dominion over some part of the world. Not only the rich and powerful but also the poor and marginalized can order and improve some part of the world. Everyone can contribute something good within their domain of influence.

Human beings have the radical power to choose in the present to bring new, good states of affairs into being that would not have existed but for their choices and actions—new human lives, new food and provisions, new customs and traditions, new institutions and associations, and new technologies and innovations. Humans have the power to create and order societies in a way analogous to the way that the God described in the Bible creates and orders the universe, with variety and beauty and good things everywhere.

Though this backstory belongs to particular monotheists, the basic lessons about human nature that this story illustrates were affirmed widely in the ancient world. Pagan Greek and Roman philosophers had neither the Jewish scriptures nor a clear picture of free choice. But they also noticed the godlike capacities of human beings to order the world in new and good ways according to reason.

Therefore, Aristotle observed that human beings are either the best of all creatures or the worst, according to whether they pursue the good and beautiful and virtuous or rather the evil and base and vicious. Cicero took this picture a step further when he remarked on the "creature of foresight, wisdom, variety, keenness, memory, endowed with reason and judgment, which we call man," who alone of all living creatures "participates in reason and reflection," a divine capacity "which, when it has developed and become complete, is rightly called wisdom."

Reading the ancient theological and philosophical texts on which our culture and laws were constructed, one repeatedly discovers the awe that people have expressed through the ages for the human capacity to bring about great goods and great evils. By choosing well and acting wisely, we are able to order the world fruitfully and beautifully. By choosing badly, we can make a hell on earth. The goal is not freedom for its own sake but rather freedom to achieve the common good.

If we return to our two colleges, we can observe that they might reasonably pursue different aspects of knowledge by different means. But the good that they are after—the pursuit of knowledge—shapes and limits what is permissible for them to do. Some acts are intrinsically wrong, such as defamation and deceit. To teach falsehoods is not a justifiable educational goal. Nor does the end of knowledge justify intrinsically wrong means. We could not justify torturing someone in order to obtain knowledge from them, for example.

Those who exercise dominion must first master themselves before they would serve as masters to guide and govern others. The object of dominion is neither mere freedom from coercion nor to exercise over others. The goal is not simply to be free to do what we want. It is to choose well, to choose the good. Humans are the authors of their actions, creators of new states of affairs, by virtue of their free choices. They are authors of *good* states of affairs by virtue of their exercise of reason, which directs them toward the common good and away from selfish gratifications. Only those who are well-practiced in the virtue of practical reason can first identify what ends are good and then strategize just and effective means of achieving good ends.

The fundamental problem is that we do not often *want* what is good. Indeed, our desires often direct us toward what is bad. We humans must employ reason to order our passions and appetites toward the good, else our passions and appetites will deflect us from doing what is right, and our reason will enable us to perpetrate greater evils. A person who does not govern his passions and appetites through right reason is enslaved to his passions and appetites and has no competence to exercise dominion over himself, much less his political community. We see this in hormonal teenagers. We see it more clearly and tragically in people who suffer addictions, who cannot control their appetites for drugs or gambling. They are not masters of their own actions. Their desires rule over them.

What is true of hormonal teenagers and addicts is true in some measure about all of us. The standing threat to good governance of the natural world is the human nature that destroys nature, the unreasoned motivation toward evil. Christian scripture and tradition teaches that this nature is within all of us and threatens to dominate us and to overwhelm our reason. Saint Paul advised the Roman Christians not to yield to vices, lest they obscure the image of God within themselves, disable their power to reason, and become like animals. And Paul taught that we all do this in some measure. We know this is wrong, Paul insists, because we have the law of reason written on our rational nature, on our souls or hearts.

Summarizing the tradition about natural law and practical reason, the philosopher John Finnis says that "one's deeds (acts, actions) are really human only if one is fully in charge—ruler, master, owner {dominus} of them." Our rational nature can direct our animal nature—our passions and appetites—toward what is good and right. This is seen clearly in the life of the family. Parenthood is the first office of dominion after one attains self-governance. Dominion starts in the family, and the family carries self-governance forward from one generation to the next. To discipline one's children is an exercise of dominion, the purpose of which is to enable one's children someday to exercise dominion over their own passions and appetites and to achieve self-governance. Without such discipline, children remain enslaved to their passions. With it, they are free to pursue excellence in whatever goals they desire to pursue.

Therefore, one must never exercise power to harm the family. To get a flourishing society, we need people who have mastered their emotions and passions. To get such people, we need parents to raise and shape the characters of their children. Thus, the family is the first and most fundamental of all domains in society. Except in cases of abuse, by right, it must remain inviolable. Anyone who wishes to help a people develop into a society, and anyone who wishes to see a flourishing society preserved from one generation to the next, must first do no harm to the natural rights and duties of marriage and parentage.

THE RESULT OF PLURAL DOMINION: THE COMMON GOOD

Dominion begins in the home but does not end there. It extends outward into greater spheres of action and influence to bring about richer and more complex goods than any individual person or family could achieve alone. The job of exercising dominion is to bring order out of chaos and to bring artificial order out of natural order, to tame the plants and animals and other natural resources, and to lay down a pattern that will bring about the common good. It is first to distinguish and discriminate according to natural kind, and then to create new orders and technologies.

In the first place, think of a farmer weeding his field, removing weeds that do not belong from among the crop. A cornfield clear of weeds is an order brought about by human dominion over the natural world. In the second place, consider an inventor who is designing a new device to till the soil more efficiently than the farmer can do by hand. A hoe and a plow are new artifacts of human creativity brought about by the exercise of dominion. The dominion that the farmer exercises over the natural world and the inventor exercises over the artifactual world feed many people. Moreover, they are beautiful.

Now property rights must come in to preserve the common good in all its diversity. This ordering cannot happen unless law stands guard around the domains of the farmer and the inventor. The law must secure the farmer's real property and the inventor's intellectual property against trespass, infringement, and other acts of theft. Otherwise, the fruits of their labor will be destroyed. Or the farmer and inventor will be deprived of their incentives to order the world in the first place.

Indeed, the first job of law is to secure the plural domains within which people exercise dominion. If each person's domain is secure against infringement by others, then we might learn to trust each other and then to negotiate with each other, to share with each other the practical wisdom we have attained. In that case, we might form more complex cooperative ventures to pursue ever more complicated goods, and even more possibilities will emerge for future choice and action.

With enough people contributing knowledge and practical wisdom, we might invent the internal combustion engine, the disc harrow, and the mechanical planter. Not only will these technologies improve the practice of agriculture and make it possible to feed more people, but the creation of such technologies will also prompt us to create new vocations and even professions, such as engineering, finance, and law. We might discover that such professions have their own, specialized knowledge and that it makes sense to build institutions that will carry the wisdom and practices of each vocation and profession from one generation to the next.

As we come to trust and rely upon each other more and specialize more precisely,[1] our efforts to order the world become efficient, and we find that we have more time to devote to the pursuit of even more precious goods, such as knowledge and beauty and play. And to enhance our realization and enjoyment of those goods, we might build other practices and institutions—schools and universities, museums and orchestras, clubs and teams. To secure our prosperous domains against aggressors, and to deter those who would steal the fruits of our labors without contributing, we might employ soldiers and sailors to guard our coasts and our lands.

Each of these domains of human choice and action is constituted by its own unique goods—food and health for the farmer, knowledge for the university, skillful practice of a particular set of techniques for the engineering and law firms and soldiers and sailors, and so on. This is the stuff of dominion. It is the stuff of being human.

Notice that we have not yet said anything about the state's dominion—government. That is because government does not produce any of these human goods. The only reason to extend dominion to the political community as a whole—that is, the only reason to have government—is to secure all of the goods that these plural and private domains produce and to protect the people and groups that produce them against wrongs. The point of political dominion is to secure our trust in each other by clarifying the rules, applying them equally to everyone, and by remedying, sanctioning, and preventing wrongs against other people and their domains. To paraphrase the American founders, to secure the natural liberties and powers that God has delegated to us to exercise dominion in the world, governments are instituted among men.

THE DOMAINS OF ORDERED LIBERTY

Just dominion requires liberty. Knowledge of what is just and right is realized when one freely chooses what is good for its own sake. Therefore, self-governance can only develop where the agent has the freedom to choose.

Nevertheless, we need someone to exercise authority. For humans, who owing to their capacity for practical reason and are the noblest of all creatures when virtuous, are also the worst of all creatures when vicious. Freedom of choice just is an opportunity both to participate in new creation and to elect to destroy what is good (which is also an opportunity to unmake one's reasonableness, to become more vicious). When we act viciously, we destroy each other's incentives for virtue. A culture conducive to vice generates more vice. The vicious man takes advantage of the virtuous man's obedience to law. Why be virtuous and obey the law if the vicious man can with impunity steal the fruits of one's labors?

For these reasons, we need law and legal judgment. To address this need, one possible solution might be to create one office of dominion over all the resources. We could place in it the person possessing the greatest practical wisdom and delegate to that person all the liberties and powers of dominion.

The practical problems with this solution are obvious. We have no guarantee that the wisest person will occupy the office. Even delegating to the second- or third-wisest person would fail to maximize our mastery over vice and chaos. And an incontinent or vicious man who occupies the office will create a hell on Earth, as the totalitarian thugs of the twentieth century demonstrated. Furthermore, power corrupts. As we saw in Chapter 8, even a virtuous or continent person is capable of doing wrong.

Moreover, even if we could design perfect political institutions that always were managed by wise people, there are more fundamental, principled reasons not to pursue centralized dominion. First, decentralized dominion is better fitting to human nature. A single plan should not be forced on everyone, even if it were the best possible plan. People should be free to develop practical reasonableness, to become more fully human. God's original delegation of dominion to human beings, described in Hebrew scriptures, is a model for human rulers and governors to imitate.

The Catechism of the Catholic Church reflects this insight by tying God's delegation of dominion to his human creatures together with the doctrine of subsidiarity. This principle means that there are inherent, principled limitations on the powers of the state.

God has not willed to reserve to himself all exercise of power. He entrusts to every creature the functions it is capable of performing, according to the capacities of its own nature. This mode of governance ought to be followed in social life. The way God acts in governing the world, which bears witness to such great regard for human freedom, should inspire the wisdom of those who govern human communities. They should behave as ministers of divine providence.

The principle of subsidiarity is opposed to all forms of collectivism. It sets limits for state intervention. It aims at harmonizing the relationships between individuals and societies. It tends toward the establishment of true international order.[2]

Furthermore, central plans are inherently incoherent. Different people and groups pursue radically different and equally basic goods, or radically different and incommensurable instantiations of the same goods (see Authenticity College and Virtue College). Dominion must be plural because basic human goods are plural. Knowledge is not reducible to liberty, which is not of the same kind of value as friendship, which is not commensurable to beauty or human life. This is why the common good of the engineering university is not the same as the common good of the liberal arts college, which is not the common good of the musical theater or the symphony orchestra, which is not the common good of the family.

Earlier chapters have addressed the growing tendencies of participants in our civic discourse to find moral fault in others. We perceive the wrongs of others and insist that our own proposals are right. Furthermore, with our inverted understanding of rights and wrongs, we are quick to complain that our own rights have been infringed and that we are entitled to the remedy that we seek. The remedies we desire are often coercive and impose our own personal conceptions of the good on others. We do not often enough consider that other, different goods might be at stake. One-size-fits-all solutions are a standing temptation.

However, the plurality of human goods means that a society cannot rationally operate on a single, unitary plan of action. Any central plan is inherently arbitrary because it requires everyone to pursue one good instead of other equally important goods. And it is unjust because it usurps the authority of people to pursue the goods toward which their own domains are oriented. The common good of the state or other political institutions has no value in itself. Its instrumental value is derived entirely from the basic goods of the various domains that it serves. Government is justified only to the extent that it protects the plural domains of society from harm and does not interfere in their good orders.

This is why the rule of law requires the government to secure, and not to abrogate, property rights. Many different and incompatible uses of resources can, with equal rationality, claim to be grounded in the pursuit of some human good or goods. It is unjust to take away from people the liberty and power to decide what is to be done with their lives and resources. A central plan deprives people of the opportunity to become self-governing people, more fully human. And it does so without reason. People must have the right, as individuals and in groups and associations, to decide what is good and right to do with the resources within their dominion. To enforce one central plan on everyone is to fail to accord equal concern and respect to the individuals and groups whose goods and plans the central plan displaces.

The product of all this is what we call civil society. Within their domains, human beings have opportunities to govern themselves and the societies of which they are part, including opportunities to determine their own rights and duties. This enables them to become practically reasonable. It also enables people to cooperate with each other to pursue complex and valuable goods. The church and the synagogue strengthen the family, and the family returns the favor. The university disseminates knowledge to the market, and the market returns resources to the university. Lenders and investors finance innovators, who improve the lives of the family, which supplies self-governing citizens to all of the other domains of society, and so on. Each domain pursues its own goods and enhances the goods of the others.

This is how human persons flourish. The plural goods pursued distinctly and in cooperative ventures by the plural domains of civil society grow the opportunities that the society provides *and simultaneously* secure the conditions in which human beings become practically reasonable and just. The job of government is first to prevent anyone from usurping the law and destroying this cooperative flourishing and, second, to refrain from causing harm itself. Government's domain is subsidiary to the domains of society, though no less important. Indeed, we could not do without it. However, it must not step over the boundaries of its own domain to stamp out the dominion of the persons for whose good it exists.

For a people to flourish in all the diverse aspects of the good they are capable of bringing about, they must be free to choose a plurality of projects. For that to happen, government and politics must be put in their place. We can lower the stakes of our public controversies, lower the temperature of our civic discourse, and avoid zero-sum contests over totalizing plans of action if we will simply allow the plural domains of society to do their work.

NOTES

1. Astute readers will recognize that the basic principles underlying this part of the story are drawn from Adam Smith, *An Inquiry into the Nature and Causes of the Wealth of Nations* (1776).
2. Catechism of the Catholic Church, §§ 1884–85.

Postscript

This bookends with a prescription for how to allow different groups to make their own rights while also prohibiting wrongs. However, most of us hope that right and wrong are not the last words. Therefore, a word must be said about another idea that goes beyond our moral disagreements, differences, sins, and failures. We long to see justice done, and we desire condemnation and remedies for wrongs committed. But that is not our final hope. We also desire something more.

Just as we see in our laws and customs reason to believe that we can know what is right to do, we also see in our laws and customs that we can forgive each other when we fail to do what is right. Our laws allow defaulting debtors to redeem their mortgages, recover their pledged assets, and even to discharge their debts in bankruptcy. Our laws also empower executive officials to pardon convicted criminals. They allow judges to suspend sentences and require judges to consider a convicted defendant's acceptance of responsibility and expression of regret when sentencing. These laws reflect our conviction that people sometimes need a second chance and, though they do not always deserve it, can be forgiven for failing to do their duty.

Our private laws and customs reflect a similar belief. Many insurance companies forgive traffic infractions and accidents after a certain number of years. Schools and universities often put students on probation for their first disciplinary offense or failure to make grades rather than dismiss the students outright. We understand that none of us is perfect. We know that each of us sometimes fails to do what is right.

Sometimes, we even do what is wrong on purpose. We are capable of evil. And yet we also know that people can regret their mistakes and their wrongs. And even evil acts can be forgiven. The Truth and Reconciliation Commission formed in South Africa after the fall of Apartheid demonstrated this possibility to the world. The Commission uncovered abhorrent acts of wrongdoing. And a nation showed that it is possible both to judge wrongdoing rightly and to forgive those who perpetrated the wrongs.

We know this also from our personal experiences and private thoughts. The experience of regret is one of the strongest pieces of evidence that we know what we must not do and can figure out what we should do. It shows that there is such a thing as right and wrong. Were there not a right thing to do, we would have no reason to regret failing to do it. Therefore, regret teaches us that we should do what is right and should judge wrongful acts as wrong. Moreover, it teaches us that people are capable of turning away from their wrongdoing and of repenting of the attitudes and intentions that led them to injure others.

Indeed, the experience of regret teaches us that we do well to forgive people for wrongs that they acknowledge and of which they repent. Someone who regrets a bad action and repents of it—who resolves not to do it again in the future—is capable of living well in community with others and doing what is right. The regretful person is qualitatively different than the person who committed a deliberate wrong but demonstrates no remorse. To forgive a wrongdoer who confesses his wrongdoing, expresses regret, and resolves not to act wrongly in the future, enables the wrongdoer to be reconciled with those he has wronged. And it makes it easier for him to do the right thing next time.

Remarkably, some people even manage to forgive wrongdoers who express no regrets, demonstrate no remorse, and never repent of their wrongdoing. A striking example of this occurred in Charleston, South Carolina. When mass-murderer Dylann Roof appeared for his bond hearing after being charged with the shooting deaths of nine people at the Emanuel African Methodist Episcopal Church, family members of the victim were given the opportunity to speak to him. They used the moment to offer their forgiveness to Roof and to urge him to repent of his wrongdoing. One of the most memorable statements came from Nadine Collier, daughter of one of the victims.

> You took something very precious away from me. I will never talk to her ever again. I will never be able to hold her again. But I forgive you and have mercy on your soul. You hurt me. You hurt a lot of people. But God forgives you, and I forgive you.

This is stern stuff, not easily understood. Where does it come from?

Christians such as these are taught Saint Paul's admonition to the Christians at Colossae, which says they should forgive one another "as the Lord forgave you." This scripture reminds Christians that we are all flawed moral beings and that we all fail. It teaches that the Son of God took upon himself the price of all our wrong actions and, thereby, enabled God to forgive us. The promise held out by people who make this claim is that anyone can find forgiveness for their sins simply by asking for it. And people who have received and experienced forgiveness (and know it) want to pass it on to others.

This does not mean that forgiveness is cheap or easy. To the contrary, it always costs someone. Moreover, it usually costs the person who was wronged. But the Christian account is that God showed us how to forgive and promised His forgiveness to all who believe in Him.

The story of how this promise of forgiveness came about is written in another book. This book should not, and likely will not, be confused for that one. Chances are, you can find a copy of it nearby.

Index

About the Author

Adam J. MacLeod is professor of law at Faulkner University, Thomas Goode Jones School of Law. A former research fellow at Princeton University and George Mason University, he is coeditor of two textbooks and author of *Property and Practical Reason* (2015) as well as dozens of articles, essays, and book reviews in academic journals and journals of popular opinion. Before teaching, MacLeod clerked for state and federal judges in Massachusetts and Colorado. He holds degrees from Gordon College and the University of Notre Dame.